Growing Old

Growing Old

NOTES ON AGING WITH
SOMETHING LIKE GRACE

Elizabeth Marshall Thomas

HarperOne
An Imprint of HarperCollins*Publishers*

HarperOne

The names and identifying details of some of the individuals in this book have been changed to protect their privacy.

FIRST EDITION

Designed by Joy O'Meara

Library of Congress Cataloging-in-Publication Data

Names: Thomas, Elizabeth Marshall, 1931- author.
Title: Growing old : notes on aging with something like grace / Elizabeth Marshall Thomas.
Description: San Francisco : HarperOne, [2020]
Identifiers: LCCN 2019016989 (print) | LCCN 2019017805 (ebook) | ISBN 9780062956439 (hardcover) | ISBN 9780062956477
Subjects: LCSH: Older women—United States—Biography. | Aging—United States. | Older people—United States—Social conditions—21st century.
Classification: LCC HQ1064.U5 T456 2019   (print) | LCC HQ1064.U5 (ebook) | DDC 305.260973—dc23
LC record available at https://lccn.loc.gov/2019016989
LC ebook record available at https://lccn.loc.gov/2019017805

20 21 22 23 24   LSC   10 9 8 7 6 5 4 3 2 1

To Stephanie and Bob
To Saibhung Singh and Saibhung Kaur
To Janice Frost and Nancy Folsom

In loving memory of my husband, Steve,
and my dear friend Anna Martin

Introduction

Why write a book about old age? Nobody wants it. Nobody likes it. When I told a friend what I was doing, she said sarcastically, "That sounds like fun," because except for senior discounts we see nothing good about it. When it comes, we try to hide it while our minds and bodies crumble, and death is our only escape.

But this view is needlessly negative. Death is the price we pay for life. Only plants, animals, fungi, and single-cell organisms have it, and all of us pay for it sooner or later. Like most of us, I see the price as extra high, something like getting a six-figure credit-card bill. Would it be nice to avoid it?

I live in rural New Hampshire, and when I looked around for a debt-free entity, I saw just grasses and trees. That didn't help—all of them will pay the price just like I will. Then I saw a stone in my field.

Three hundred million years ago, about ten miles below the earth's surface, this stone was formed. Somehow it got squeezed up and out, and in 10,000 BC a glacier brought it to the place where I saw it. By then it was 29 million years old. What's that like? You see what it's like if you imagine time as distance and picture the time between now and 10,000 BC as one foot on a very long ruler; the rock was formed five miles away on that ruler.

In 1935 my father brought me to the same place. I was four years old and since then I've seen some changes. The trees are taller, a pond appeared when my dad made a dam in a stream, and the town paved the dirt road that went by our house. All that was quite something, especially the road, because soon after it was paved, the town gave it a different name. This took emotional adjustment on our part.

But consider the stone. Assuming it popped from the earth in a good place and had consciousness, it could have watched evolution transform a single-cell organism into a Tyrannosaurus rex and later watched another dinosaur transform into a bird. With life and consciousness, the stone could have known what influenced these transformations—the climate changes, the great extinctions, and the great recoveries. Just in my area it would have seen the glacier melting, the frozen earth recovering, plants starting to grow, and wildlife starting to flourish.

Mammoths and cave lions passed by this stone. Penacook and Abenaki people camped near it. European settlers arrived, built a house and a barn, and cut down hundreds of trees to make the field.

This last is but a nanosecond in the stone's long existence. Even the scientists will never know what the stone could have known if it had life and consciousness. But as far as the stone is concerned, nothing has happened. It doesn't even know when it rains.

IF YOU CAN IMAGINE EXISTING FOR THREE HUNDRED MILLION years without knowing that you did so, I think you might agree that life with a price seems better than eternal existence for free. Our kind, the living organisms, have existed as such for as long as the stone, but unlike the stone we don't keep the same forms. We improve our species by reproducing ourselves, often without replicating ourselves exactly, and the little changes give natural selection unlimited opportunities to fix us. Thus, like the stone, we life-forms are still on earth after three billion years, but our journey was more exciting. Every one of our lives was a little window to the world with all its activity and attraction.

To be alive is to experience, and throughout our lives we

gain experience, beginning with birth, which if we're humans is when we slide from a tight, wet, warm environment into a vast, almost empty, chilly environment with air, light, scent, and sound all around us and big scary creatures looming over us. As for information, at this time in our lives we're just a tad more aware than the stone.

The end of our journey appears as we age, having collected a mixture of facts, friends, relatives, mistakes, triumphs, tragedies, and possessions. Thus old age is a predeath transition, and how we perceive it can depend on how far life has brought us.

When we're young, death and those approaching it seem to have little to do with us. Old people don't look or act like us—they might almost be a different species. As for death, we don't want it of course, but why worry about it? It seldom happens to young people. We can freely do dangerous things.

These illusions are beneficial. Why get preoccupied with old age and death before you're forced to face them? I'm already old, but if I live as long as my mother lived, to just shy of 104, what would my life have been like if I'd started to worry when I was twenty?

By middle age we've learned more. We may be only in our fifties, but we know about aging and we're saying we're not as young as we used to be. We're paying more attention to what we eat and how we exercise.

Twenty-five years later, we realize we were spring chickens while having such thoughts, because by then we're approaching the old-age transition. *Gosh, this is different.* Do we feel the transition? We can't run fast and we're careful climbing stairs, but we're still living, so we're lucky. But maybe we're starting to feel unlucky. Living like this? You call this lucky? We're prejudiced against old age.

Hopefully, this book will help with the prejudice. It mentions the rough parts of aging, but only to tell the whole story. So it's totally truthful, and it points out the good parts too. Some of these may come as surprises, because we may not realize what they arc or see them as good. If we retire from a job we liked, for instance, we may fail to see our new freedom as an opportunity to do some of the things we never had time to do when we were working. Of course we must adjust as best we can, but knowing what's coming can help us prepare and understand.

PLENTY OF BOOKS HAVE BEEN WRITTEN ABOUT AGING, BUT MOST are by practicing doctors who observed their geriatric patients, analyzing the medical, social, and behavioral factors, usually with suggestions for making the process go smoothly. Many of these books are well worth reading—*Being Mortal* by Atul Gawande is outstanding—but these books were written by authors whom I'd consider young. They saw what aging could do, but they couldn't have known what it's like.

They remind me of a good friend who, when in her twenties, wrote a health column for a newspaper. "Health" included aging, and her readers didn't like bad news, so she wrote about ninety-year-olds who hiked the Appalachian Trail and had wonderful sexual experiences. She never mentioned the eighty-year-olds who fell down flights of stairs, maybe breaking their bones or wetting their pants as they tumbled. To some extent, the abovementioned books resemble my friend's column. They try to counter our anti-aging prejudice and tend to present aging as pleasant if you do the right things.

This book is different. I'm not a physician with a degree in geriatrics; I'm a widowed great-grandmother, eighty-seven years old, who knows what aging feels like and how we elderly are viewed. For instance, it wouldn't surprise me to learn that you, the reader, got a little flash of aversion when you saw the words "widowed great-grandmother" and "eighty-seven years old."

It's a common reaction. Many younger people don't really like old people, but this isn't a popularity contest. I'm presenting a firsthand nonfiction account, some of it from my own experience. Few if any other books are like it, and considering what's in this one, that's no surprise.

But please don't assume that it's all bad news—old age has certain advantages. What about senior discounts? I got one when licensing two dogs. The licenses cost $6.50 per dog, so I would have paid $13.00, but seniors get a $4.50 discount for one dog, so I paid just $8.50. And because I've been buying things all my life and now have everything I need plus piles of things I no longer use, I don't need to buy much else.

In addition to senior discounts and owning lots of possessions, you also have more time to yourself. I've had more time to enjoy my grandchildren. When I was younger, I didn't even have grandchildren. And you might enjoy experiences that may once have seemed routine. These days my favorite experience is going to bed. The two little dogs and my three cats want to come with me. We walk down a hall to the bedroom together, the dogs first, me next, the cats following. The dogs sleep close to me under the covers and the cats sleep on top of us. The bed is a single-bed cot so it gets crowded, but we like being close together.

The old-age transition has downsides too, such as loss of memory and crumbling bones. On this I'm well informed and will offer examples, such as losing my car key permanently or falling and breaking my hip.

Certain problems bring us to hospitals or to companies that provide home care for elders, so for information about these I enlisted the help of three nurses. They care for the elderly and they're good friends, so at my request they described certain hospitals and care-providing companies, pointing out the benefits but also the unwelcome events and conditions. These women could be fired if the managers knew everything they told me, so here I don't use their names. All facts are important, not just good facts. I tell the whole story when I can.

That's one reason I'm writing this book. And I have another reason. The books I wrote before I was old were mostly about the natural world or about humans with lifestyles more vigorous than ours. This often required risky or strenuous research, and I'm too old for that now.

I began researching in the 1950s when I was in my early twenties, living among the San (formerly known as Bushmen) in what is now Namibia. These people are known to be the first people and thus are our ancestors. Those we met were precontact hunter-gatherers in a vast "unexplored" area of southern Africa, about 120,000 square miles known to white people as "the end of the earth." We stayed mostly within an area the San called Nyae Nyae—6,000 square miles in the southern part of that vast space.

I put quotes around "unexplored," because that's what white people called it, and white people overrate themselves. The residents knew every inch of it, as suggested by an archaeological study of one of their encampments showing continuous occupancy for eighty-five thousand years. I spent about three of those years among these wonderful people and wrote my first book about them. The title is my translation of *Ju/'hoansi,** their name for themselves. *Ju* means "person," */'hoan* means "pure" or "safe," and *si* makes it plural. I translated this as *The Harmless People*. When I was older I wrote another book about them, *The Old Way: A Story of the First People*, and because I was older and also much wiser, *The Old Way* is probably better.

For another project, I walked seventy-five miles across Baffin Island to visit a den of wolves. There, I spent the Arctic summer alone in a little cave as I watched them, and because

---

* The / indicates a click made with the tongue at the side of the mouth.

wolves became dogs, I described these wolves when I wrote *The Hidden Life of Dogs*.

I also lived in northern Uganda among warlike pastoralists known as Dodoth. This resulted in a book called *Warrior Herdsmen*. The only encounter I've had with a celebrity took place there—I unexpectedly met Idi Amin, then an officer in the King's African Rifles.

I was camped in the bushland near the escarpment that forms the border with Kenya, and one morning he arrived at my camp in a truck filled with soldiers. They marched down the escarpment into Kenya where, I later learned, they killed all the people in the nearest village, wrongly believing that the men of this village had stolen cattle in Uganda.

The soldiers returned with the burned corpse of one of their victims, which, for an unknown reason, Idi Amin wanted moved to a government post forty miles to the south. Understandably, he didn't want to take it himself, so he came striding up to me and ordered me to take it.

My children were with me, ages three and four. Should I take them on a forty-mile ride with a corpse or leave them behind with Idi Amin? Cell phones weren't available then, so no one could warn the Uganda officials. I wasn't sure what they'd think if a foreign white woman who looked like a tourist drove up with the burned corpse of a man from Kenya in the trunk.

Playing the part of a weak little woman, chin low, eyes blinking, I told him my car wasn't strong—not like his truck. And I wasn't a good driver like him and his men. The road was just a track, I said. I wasn't sure how to drive on it, and I was truly sorry. This made him angry, but he bought it. He and the soldiers went west in their truck. I sat down and breathed deeply.

Now my ability to do such things is gone. My mind doesn't work as well as it did, and I've lost most of my strength. I'd get chest pains if asked to transport a burned corpse. I might even faint if I saw it. And I couldn't walk across Baffin Island. Ever since I broke my hip, I sometimes take wobbly steps, so I might fall down and couldn't get up. A polar bear might find me and eat me. The wolves I wanted to visit might eat me. I'd meet my death before I died of something else, or sooner than I expected.

So here I am, alone in my kitchen. Will anyone find this of interest? They won't if I write about what I'm doing, like looking out the window to see if a deer is in my field. I'm doing that now in rural New Hampshire, and there isn't a deer in the field. But I've had quite a life, all things considered. So far it's been with me for thirty-one thousand days—and to review thirty-one thousand days of anyone's life as it trudges toward the finish line might very well be of interest.

The aging process is an essential part of the human story, and it's not for the faint-hearted. It's as strange as it is captivating—a venture to the unknown.

One

The average age of our species is thirty. That's the average age worldwide. Thus most people on our planet—more than seven billion of them—don't have a clue about aging. They're like me when I was thirty, when old age was a far-off event that I knew might happen sometime, but so what? My parents and their friends weren't old when I was thirty, and my two grandmothers, by then deceased, were already old when I knew them. They lived with us, and every day they'd look the same as they did the day before, so they didn't appear to be aging. Even so, because my grandmothers had always been old as far as I knew and I had always been young, old age seemed like a rare condition I didn't need to think about.

I think about it now, though. Space travel must be something like it. But one slides into it quietly. It's not startling like, say, the shock you'd feel if you saw a lion's shining eyes as you sat at night by your campfire. It's more like wandering around a shopping plaza, looking for the supermarket in a setting that seems familiar, except you're not sure you recognize everything you see. Have they changed things around here, or are you in the wrong place? You don't have an iPhone with a GPS because those are for young people. You don't really know what "GPS" means, and you wouldn't know how to use one if you did. But a man is walking toward you. Perhaps he can give you directions.

Normally he'd look at you, and so he does, or at least he looks in your direction, but his gaze slides away. The sight of an elderly woman didn't register with him. You haven't been old very long, so this surprises you. You seem not to be living in a world you know.

Yet while looking at the man, you see behind him. There you see the supermarket. You've been going the wrong way. So you go to the market and do your shopping. Luck is with you—you remembered to bring your shopping list. And as you walk along the aisles, you remember you need cat food. This isn't on your list, but your mind is clear when it comes to your cat. You easily remember which foods he likes, and you put ten cans of his favorites in your shopping cart.

That afternoon, your neighbor comes to your door, bringing a jar of soup. You don't know why. She brought it because everyone knows that elderly people living alone find it hard to care for themselves. She wants to help you, and she hands you the soup, smiling.

You're not sure what to do with it, but you thank her and invite her to come in. She sits on your sofa, and your cat jumps up beside her. Your neighbor doesn't like cats. She shoves him off the sofa. But he lands on his feet as he always does, and he comes to sit on your lap.

You're too polite to reprimand your neighbor, but you don't like to see your cat mistreated, so you stroke him to console him while you offer your neighbor some tea. She declines and then starts talking.

She asks if you're in good health, you tell her you are, and then she talks about the weather; but she's visiting you because you're old, and her talk turns to the other old people she knows. She reveals their medical issues—one has arthritis, another has osteoporosis, and a third is getting dementia. You also have arthritis, and when you express your sympathy, your neighbor sees she just reminded you that your body is failing. She chooses a more appropriate topic. "My grandmother is ninety-three," she says brightly. "My great-aunt lived to ninety-eight."

You ponder this. When you were in your thirties, your neighbors didn't tell you they knew people in their forties. Your neighbor sees you as a walking cadaver—her demise isn't imminent, but yours is. Her great-aunt didn't *die* at ninety-eight;

she *lived* to ninety-eight because your neighbor wants to encourage you. *You mustn't worry about dying soon, although you're going to*, she's saying.

The problem doesn't end here, of course—now and then you need a little help. After a snowfall, for instance, she sees you trying to shovel your walkway and she sends her husband to do it for you. The snow is wet and heavy; your arthritic joints are starting to ache. Your neighbor is a good, kind person, and her husband is too. When he asks for the shovel, you're grateful, and you thank him.

Evening comes. You watch TV. You see an ad that shows two bathtubs in the woods, a naked man in one and a naked woman in the other. They're not old like you—no one would buy the advertised product if recommended by people with gray hair and wrinkles. Instead, both are in early middle age, and they're happy with what they're promoting. It's a drug called Cialis, for erectile dysfunction, and they're smiling at each other because their sex life is improving, but somehow this escapes you. What do bathtubs have to do with anything? And why did these people put them in the woods? Where do they get the hot water? You seem to be missing something.

The puzzle stays vaguely in your mind until bedtime. You turn down the heat, and your furnace falls silent. You check the doors to make sure they're locked. You check the lights to make sure they're off. You check the coffee machine to make sure it's unplugged, because a machine can start a fire if it's powered. Often enough, you wake in the morning to find you haven't done one or more of those things, so you stand still for a moment, considering. Yes, this time you've done all of them.

You put on your nightgown and brush your teeth. You take your pills—lots of them—not only vitamins but also medications to strengthen your bones and help with your arthritis. You take a laxative to keep your colon functioning. You take a homeopathic pill to help you sleep naturally. Then you lie down on your bed.

Your cat has been watching. When you pull up the covers and turn off the light, you feel his little whiskers tickling your nose. He rubs his cheek on yours. He presses against your shoulder, purring. That you are eighty years his senior means nothing to either of you, and for the first time that day you smile a beaming, spontaneous smile because he's purring. You belong to each other. You both feel loved. You both feel peaceful. You are the most important mortals in each other's lives.

Two

As we age, we experience changes, and perhaps the most dramatic is in our sense of time. When we were young, time crawled along slowly, but as we start aging, it flies. One day in 2016 a friend came to my house with a book I'd written and asked me to sign it. As I did, she asked when it was published. I was then eighty-five and felt it was published recently but couldn't remember just when. So I opened the book to find the copyright and saw it was published in 1993, or twenty-three years earlier.

To me, that seemed like yesterday. But yesterday I'd been doing errands, so I began to think back, wondering what I'd been doing in 1993. Of course, I didn't remember, so I thought about the meaning of twenty-three years, wondering what this time period would show me.

The truth came as a surprise. During my first experience with a twenty-three-year time period, I learned to walk, learned to talk, went to elementary school, learned to read and write, went to high school, learned to drive, started college, met a nice man, lived for a while in the Kalahari Desert (in Namibia), came home, finished college, was given a Volkswagen bug by my father, married the nice man, and went to live in North Carolina, driving the Volkswagen bug all the way from my parents' home in Cambridge, Massachusetts, because my new husband had been drafted and was stationed at Fort Bragg.

There I got a job as a secretary in a school for disabled African American children. I'm a white person, and North Carolina, like South Africa, had apartheid, so my employment by black people annoyed some other white folks so much that, as I stepped off a sidewalk to cross the street one morning, one of them tried to run over me with his car. I jumped back on the sidewalk and dashed into a store, where I waited until he was out of sight. So I'm here to tell the story. When I told it to some white people in North Carolina, none were surprised.

All these experiences were life-changing. They moved me from being one kind of person to being another—from being illiterate, say, to being a reader, from being trustful to being suspicious, as I was when I saw the white man looking at me while turning his car in my direction. If I had to explain the importance of these experiences, I'd need to write a book for each one.

But now my sense of time seems different, as do my learning experiences. When I saw the date of the copyright, I felt that the book, which wasn't my first, was just one among thousands of other published books, and publication was no more than a normal event that happens from time to time and doesn't make much difference. Friends and family members died, all to my infinite sorrow, but these deaths didn't change my life except for the death of my husband, and even then I managed to trudge forward as if I was dealing with it. My daily life stayed more or less the same.

THUS, IN MY FIRST TWENTY-THREE YEARS I HAD DOZENS, MAYBE hundreds, of important experiences that changed who I was and what I did. Others that changed me, such as having children, doing research in the Arctic and in various parts of Africa, working for the embassy of the State of Kuwait, having grandchildren, writing more books, and teaching in various universities and in a maximum-security prison, all took place between the late 1950s and the time the abovementioned book was published.

But in those last twenty-three years, I've had just one life-changing experience. And this, of all things, concerned commas. The giant flash of insight about the use of commas didn't change the way I lived—it wasn't like learning to drive—and perhaps a reader won't find this impressive. Perhaps that reader is young and doesn't understand that we elders are set in our ways or that an experience of this kind is a revelation, and the only reason it doesn't change our lives is because it's mental, with nothing physical to show for it except the commas themselves. Here's what happened.

For most of my life I saw the comma as an unwanted contrivance of the punctuation police, invented so that editors could irritate writers by splattering commas on their manuscripts. I used fairly few commas, and when I'd submit a manuscript to a publisher, the editor would add dozens more, which I would scratch out, writing "STET" wherever I did. To me, the added commas were a time-consuming nuisance and "STET" was a wonderful word, if known only to editors and writers, meaning "leave it as it is."

But for two of my books, I encountered unusually reasonable editors who weren't just following self-created rules that mess up a manuscript but could show the purpose of every comma on a page. Their edits too had several new commas, but both times I thought carefully as I read, taking time to evaluate each comma, absorbing how it felt in the sentence and sensing its value.

Now I'm a comma expert. If you disagree with a particular comma or with the number of commas in this book, please understand that although some are here to satisfy the punctuation police; most of them are here to create a little thought pause as you're reading. This book has 3,388 commas, and each fulfills its mission. Here, an old dog learned a new trick, and today you will find her carefully considered commas on every page.

See the comma after "trick"? It's nice. Your mind paused before you read further, just as it should. I could write three more pages about why that comma matters, but since this could be distracting, I'll save the information for the four-hundred-page book entitled *Commas* I plan to write when I'm older. I may even explore the question of the semicolon; I put only a few in this book because I haven't considered them yet, or not fully, and possibly I'm wrong about the one I just used. Maybe I should think more about it. A period might have been better.

"THAT'S ALL YOU LEARNED IN TWENTY-THREE YEARS?" YOUNG people may ask, and may find the answer gloomy. But when you're my age, your opinions are solid. It's a stirring experience to change them. The young will see what I mean as they grow old, which they'll do if they're lucky.

I once said that to a much younger man, and he screamed with disbelief, "If I'm *lucky*?"

"You're lucky if you live that long," I explained. "Take me, for instance. I'll never die young."

Young people don't seem to grasp remarks like this. He scoffed and said, "You don't know that." But by then I'd already lived for eighty-two years, so I did know that.

As has been said, time flies when you're old, but to what destination? Here's the part that's worrisome, because at least in my case it's flying toward a grave in New Hampshire. This should concern me more than it does, but for some reason it doesn't, or not yet. I seem to view death as I once viewed aging—it's far away until it happens, and anyway I'm ready.

I've done the premortem jobs such as making a trust and a will, and a headstone is in place with my husband's and my name on it atop a grave in one of our town's cemeteries. My husband's name has the dates of his birth and death below it. My name has just the date of birth, but space for the death date is ready. My parents are in the same grave under the same headstone, as are the ashes of our dogs, if without headstones. And if all goes well, my ashes will be there too.

I'd tell you which cemetery, but in most states including New Hampshire state law for cemeteries forbids the remains of nonhumans. Most people don't know this—it's been my impression that quite a few people are buried with their dogs, just as they should be, and I'm sure the families of those people didn't know it was illegal. I even met a funeral director who didn't know the law, and often enough, at a family's request, she'd put the remains of pets in the coffins with their owners.

Some people know the law but ignore it, considering it to be New Hampshire's construction of hell. I had to ignore it, because my parents were in the grave before I learned about it, and my husband and I had planned to be with them. As far as we were concerned, our dogs were our close relatives, but even so, on the day we buried my husband's ashes, I felt a little nervous. What if someone from the cemetery saw what we were doing?

We were lucky. When the kind gentleman who opens graves for people saw me with two bags of ashes—my husband's and the dogs'—and knew I had arranged to bury only one, he looked at both bags and smiled at me, nodding politely. Then he got back in his truck, perhaps so we could see he wasn't watching. Perhaps he also thought the law was callous.

WE'VE HAD THIS GRAVE SINCE 1963. I WAS THIRTY-TWO WHEN I bought it. One of our closest friends died unexpectedly, her family had no grave site, and knowing we'd all need one sooner or later, I went to find two sites side by side, big enough for both families.

Our town has four cemeteries, and for no real reason I looked at three of them including the oldest, by now near the center of town because the town has grown around it. There, most graves date from about 1800 to 1930, suggesting that the process of selecting graves has gone on for a long time in New Hampshire. Many are the graves of children, and not many people lived beyond their sixties. Many of the names on the gravestones are also the names of town roads, which reminded me of my long-ago childhood, when these roads were essentially long unpaved driveways named for the people whose farms were at the ends of them. The family of one of my neighbors is still remembered here; their farm was on the road that bears their name, and their primary grave with a towering headstone is dated 1810.

That cemetery seemed to be full—not that I'd have chosen it because it's right on the road—so I chose another, and there I found the sites I wanted on the north side of a hill.

Not only were the two sites big, which was good, but bears sometimes hibernate in such places, which also is good. Needless to say, in New Hampshire the sun is always in the south—more so in winter—and south-facing places change temperature as the sun burns down. You can see what sunlight does when you're driving in winter on a country road. Where trees shade the road, it's white with snow. Where no trees shade it, you see the pavement. Some bears make their dens on the north sides of hills, perhaps because they've found that temperature change disturbs their hibernation.

Bears are not the only ones who like such places. Later, a fox made a little den by our grave site, and lilies of the valley grow there, not planted by people but growing there by their own choice. Here, the earth is home to many, so when I think of our grave, I think of a poem I was forced to read for an English class in college. To my surprise, I was smitten by it and have remembered it ever since. It's "The Night Is Freezing Fast," by A. E. Housman, and it's about his friend Dick, who killed himself.

Here's the last part, and I didn't need to look it up. After sixty-seven years, it's still in the front of my brain.

Fall, winter, fall; for he,
Prompt hand and headpiece clever,
Has woven a winter robe,
And made of earth and sea
His overcoat forever,
And wears the turning globe.

To wear the turning globe now seems consoling, but it didn't always. My first experience with death came eighty-two years ago when I was five, and here the issue of time returns because I get no signal that time has passed. When I remember what I'm about to describe, it seems to have happened this morning.

Three

I was in my parents' bathtub, chest-deep in warm water, playing with a little floating toy. I had several such toys, so I don't remember which one, but I see the rest as clearly as if it just happened.

The door was open to my parents' bedroom, where my dad was answering the phone. Soon I heard his low voice saying sadly to my mother, "Cousin Emily died."

"She died?" asked my mom.

"Last night," said my dad, almost whispering.

I listened with amazement. I'd never heard of Cousin Emily or heard my parents speak so sadly, but I knew what "died" meant and realized this had happened to someone. I burst into tears.

My parents heard me crying and came to the bathroom. "What's the matter?" asked my dad, surprised.

"She died," I sobbed, and my parents looked at each other.

"You never met her," said my dad.

"You didn't know her," said my mother.

"She lived in Nova Scotia," said my dad.

They seemed annoyed by my crying, so I tried to stop. But I will always remember that moment. For some reason I tipped my head back to look up at the shower faucet, although when I heard the news, I'd been looking straight ahead at the floating toy. My mind's eye still sees the shower faucet, alone, up high, with the tub's white waterproof lining around it. I have no idea why I looked up or why I remember this so clearly, but eighty-four years later when making a guess, I'd say I was thinking of heaven.

I WAS CONFUSED ABOUT HEAVEN. SUPPOSEDLY IT WAS A GOOD place in the sky where you went when you died, but this was open to question. Both my grandmothers lived with us, and my father's mother, Nana, was an evangelical fundamentalist Christian who believed you go to hell unless you're "born again" by accepting Christ as your Savior.

Saying "Okay, I accept that" wasn't enough. You had to experience a deep, sudden realization. Unless you have this, you're not saved, heaven is closed to you, and you burn in the fires of hell for all eternity.

I'd wonder about people all over the world who never heard of Jesus, also about people who died before he was born. Were they in hell?

Nana wasn't sure but didn't think so—they might be judged by their deeds, she said. But we know about Jesus, she'd tell us. He died to save us from being punished for the sins of human-kind. And a day didn't pass without her begging us to have the sudden flash that showed we understood this.

Back when Jesus was living, animals were sacrificed to satisfy whatever gods were up there. Our God wanted something sac-rificed to him, and it seems that an animal wasn't enough—he wanted his own son, the world's best person, killed on our behalf to save not only the sinners of the time, but also the sinners of the future. That's how bad we are, and we'll be horribly punished unless we get a deep, awesome realization that Jesus, who him-self did nothing wrong, was tortured and killed for what the rest of us are doing.

Our beloved Nana believed this deeply—religion was the focus of her life. She knew she'd be in heaven because she was saved, as would my father, she said, who must have been saved as a child, because no child could resist such constant, passion-ate pressure from his mother.

It was a childhood moment for him, though. He didn't retain it and never mentioned it in all the years I knew him. But this didn't matter, and if he sinned he would go to heaven anyway, because once you're saved you stay saved, forgiven not only for what you've done but also for what you do later.

However, the rest of us—me, my little brother, and our mother—were not saved, and Nana knew that we would go to hell. A less generous, less loving person might have said to herself, *I'm saved, my only child is saved, and if these others won't listen, let them burn.*

But our Nana was as loving and generous as it's possible to be. A day didn't pass without her begging us to accept the sacrifice of Jesus, and I, for one, would gladly have done so, but I didn't know how to get the flash. You couldn't force it—it was supposed to hit like a lightning bolt. This never happened, so I knew I was going to hell.

Hellfire didn't worry me too much. If you were dead you might not feel it, or after you were burned to ashes, your ashes wouldn't feel it, or if you just suffered and didn't turn to ashes, you'd have all eternity to adjust.

But separation from my dad was horrifying. I didn't think much of a god who would do this. If God was all-powerful, why did he let people sin? Couldn't he stop us from sinning rather than torturing us after we did?

And if we sinned, why didn't God just make us sick? Wasn't God supposed to love us, and wasn't he the model for morality? How would he feel if one of us humans did what he was doing, tearing children and their mothers away from their fathers and throwing them into a terrible fire to suffer agonizing pain?

World War II had started. Couldn't God distinguish between Hitler and my little brother? It seemed that he couldn't. If Nana had it right, he'd punish them both the same way, and he wouldn't even punish Hitler if Hitler got saved. And what about my mother? Was she the same as Hitler? The only sin she ever committed was to leave a light on in a closet after she went to bed.

And how could our dad enjoy heaven if we were being tortured? Our dad wouldn't let this happen. He would come down to hell and find us and take us to a place that wasn't in heaven or in hell where we would be together.

MY PARENTS WEREN'T RELIGIOUS. THEY DIDN'T GO TO CHURCH OR refer to the Bible. All they did about religion was to fall politely silent and look down at their hands while Nana said a lengthy grace at mealtimes.

I've never been religious. I was very young when Nana's views were presented to me, but not too young to have doubts, and by the time I was in my teens, I'd decided that if God does unacceptable things, he's not like an employer whose job you can quit or a public official you can vote against. All you can do about a cruel invisible tyrant is to believe he doesn't exist.

As for death itself, while sitting in the bathtub, listening to my father as he spoke on the phone, I knew that death was bad. After I learned I was going to hell, I thought that death was horrible, and no wonder people feared it. Later, after I learned a bit about the world, I didn't see where hell could be unless it was in the center of the earth—you're *up* in heaven or *down* in hell—and somehow I'd learned the earth's core was burning. But how would we get there? Was there a tunnel? Nobody ever mentioned a tunnel. So I decided there wasn't a hell, and death seemed a little less horrible.

Now I see death as normal. I know I'll have an afterlife, if not a conscious one. My ashes will be mixed with those of my dogs and my family. Maybe some of our molecules will get into the seeds of a nearby plant. Maybe the seeds will be eaten by a mouse who will be eaten by a fox. We won't be aware of these transitions, but even while we're living, we're unaware of most of what's happening around us, and when we're in molecular form, we will neither know nor care. What's wrong with that?

Four

Now that we're on the issue of death, we see it in two ways. Many or even most of us don't exactly fear it, myself included, which is why I presented myself as I did in the previous chapter, not minding that I'll soon be a collection of molecules buried in the graveyard dirt. To believe you'll be in heaven is probably better and certainly more optimistic, but the result is the same—dying is natural, it happens to every living organism, and it comes when it comes, so why worry?

This is the feeling we're aware of. This is in our conscious minds. But our minds have a deeper part, the unconscious part, where we keep the knowledge we gathered during our evolutionary past. This knowledge is from the natural world, so the deep, quiet part of our brain takes death more seriously.

In the natural world, few animals die of old age because most are killed in fights or by predators who eat us or by starvation if we don't get enough to eat, which is a constant problem for every wild creature. If you live in the natural world, unless you're an apex predator, too big for anyone else to damage (which we weren't), you must keep your predators in mind at all times, because if you don't, you'll be one of their victims. Most living creatures from buffaloes to houseflies are born with this knowledge, and our species is born with it too.

Have you ever watched a bird watching a snake? Or a squirrel watching a cat? The eyes of the potential victim are intensely focused on the potential predator. The snake and the cat are impending death, and their potential victims watch them with total, focused attention. Those who don't focus on what they should fear are removed from the breeding population; thus all of us have ancestors who focused, and their ability has passed on to us.

Consider our fear of the dark. Children have it, often quite openly, and although most adults overcome it, have you ever noticed a tiny squirt of relief when you enter your dark house at night and turn on the light? *Careful now*, says the instinct. *You don't know what's in here.* We trust the instinct and reach for the light switch, and the light shows us we're safe.

Lions seem to have caused this.* They don't have much luck when hunting in the daytime or on moonlit nights because their prey can see them, but after the moon is full and rising later every night, lions are seriously hungry, darkness hides them, and we are easy prey. Even now, in areas with lions, these nights are by far the most dangerous. This has been so for thousands of years and is ongoing.

Lions were our main predators, but not our only predators. Before the modern lions appeared, a giant lion type called *Dinofelis* ("terrible cat") preyed upon our ancestors. Leopards and hyenas preyed on us too, but sometimes you can beat off a hyena or even a leopard. Lions were the real problem. After all, for most of our existence we were just another mammal on the African savanna, and a midsized one at that.

Thus, ever since we came down from the trees, we've had predators, and still do in some places. That's why, somewhere in our minds, an animate predator remains. Some form of this appears in many cultures, and in ours he's a humanlike figure with a skeleton face, dressed in a black cape, carrying a scythe. He's called the Grim Reaper, and he has a scythe rather than the shining eyes of a lion or a *Dinofelis*, because his image

---

* From an important study, Craig Packer et al., "Fear of Darkness, the Full Moon and the Nocturnal Ecology of African Lions," *PLoS One* 6/7 (2011): e22285.

was conjured after the Neolithic, when our important foods were grains that are killed when a reaper harvests them. Well, they're not really killed because their roots are still functioning, but they seem to be killed by the reaper.

As a snake fascinates a bird, so the Grim Reaper fascinates us, and he does so in various ways. A friend who worked in a funeral home and lived upstairs in the building told me that morbidly curious visitors would ask to see a dead person, lie in a coffin, or see what embalming is like. Someone who had watched the television series *Six Feet Under* asked her if it was true that the dead can have erections and bowel movements. My friend said she'd never seen a corpse with an erection, but she'd seen dead people produce bowel movements. Evidently certain parts of our bodies keep functioning after our hearts and brains give up, not realizing that the organism they're trying to serve is dead and they will soon die too. People would ask my friend what happens after death, as if someone who deals with it so openly is somehow part of it.

Consider the popularity of murder mysteries and the hundreds of films and television programs that involve death. Even much of the news is about deaths caused by murderers, accidents, fires, and floods, and the reports usually continue until the perpetrator, whether a hurricane or a terrorist, has left or was removed.

We're fascinated and we're uneasy, just as the bird is uneasy when watching the snake, and our feelings show in our language. It's fine to say, "Hitler is dead," because Hitler was evil.

But when it comes to friends and family, "passed away" is softer and better, as are "no longer living," "departed," "in a better place," or "with the Lord."

A deceased individual is "the late Mr. Jones," never "the dead Mr. Jones." And interestingly, it seems harsh to say, "He's dead," but soft to say, "He died." Perhaps that's because "He's dead" implies "now," and "He died" is in the past. The predator who caused this has gone.

THE FEELINGS SHOWN BY THIS CAUTIOUS LANGUAGE MAY CON-tribute to our spending a fortune on creams that fix wrinkles, pastes that whiten teeth, and dozens of other anti-aging products. Some of us have face-lifts, and many dye their hair when it gets gray.

As for me, although I like old faces, probably because my grandmothers had them and I loved my grandmothers, I sometimes try to minimize the appearance of aging by standing up straight when I'm walking. We elders often walk with our heads low, leaning forward, and if we raise our chins and straighten our backs, we remove some of the "old" signal. I don't know why I do this, but I assume it's because, like everyone else, in the back of my mind I carry our prehistoric past, when predators chose those who seemed feeble.

Our conscious minds want us to look younger or more handsome or more beautiful. But why is this better than looking old? Because fear of death is always with us, hiding inside us, not making us cowardly, just making us sensible. All animals fear death—even insects fear death—and do what they can to avoid it.

WHAT IF THEY CAN'T? I'VE SEEN FOUR AMAZING REACTIONS, each showing an emotion we might feel in a similar situation. One involved a squirrel, another involved a raccoon, the third involved a vole, and the fourth involved a lion.

As for the squirrel, I was driving at about thirty miles an hour on a two-lane country road when the squirrel tried to cross the road in front of me. When he saw my car rushing toward him and knew the end had come, he covered his eyes with his hands.

Another time when I was driving on this road, a raccoon ran out of the bushes in front of me. He also saw he was about to be crushed, and he covered his eyes with his hands.

The vole was in a corner of my porch with two of my cats approaching from either side. She couldn't escape, she knew the cats would kill her, and she covered her eyes with her hands.

The lion was a full-grown adolescent who had been with his pride when he was shot but not killed by a farmer. Because this happened on a dark night, the farmer was afraid to follow him and finish him off, as a wounded lion at large was considered dangerous. So the task was left to my brother and a friend, who were braver than the farmer. They set out on foot with a flashlight and a rifle, and I went along. We found the injured lion lying in some bushes. He'd heard us coming, and he was watching us. When our friend raised the rifle, the lion turned his head and shut his eyes.

I SAVED THE SQUIRREL AND THE RACCOON BY SPINNING MY CAR into the left lane. Luckily, no car was coming. The squirrel continued his rush across the road, and the raccoon went back in the bushes. I saved the vole by running toward my cats, who both turned to look at me. The vole saw she had a chance and dashed away between them.

I couldn't save the lion. More than sixty years later, my mind's eye still sees him. He had been with a group of other lions and the farmer shot another lion first, so the young lion knew what a rifle was and knew what was going to happen.

Five

For me, old age as a dangerous disease stays somewhere in my brain, a nuisance that began when I was in my late forties, about to be in my early fifties, which seemed old at the time. It was then I began adding a year to my age, so on my birthday I'd be comfortable with the new number rather than stricken by it.

I've done that ever since. At the time of this writing I say I'm eighty-eight, even though I'm really eighty-seven, and on my birthday when I'll really be eighty-eight, which is pretty close to ninety, I'll be used to the idea and can prepare for being eighty-nine. Maybe I'll even say I'm ninety, because while eighty-nine is old, ninety is really, really old and could take two years to adjust to. Ninety looks to me like fifty did when I was in my forties.

Why do this when death doesn't concern me, or so I believe? Maybe death isn't the problem. Maybe I want to slow my deterioration by being younger than I say I am. Maybe if I'm still okay at eighty-seven, I'll be okay at eighty-eight, and pretending I'm there already might assure this.

Reality can be disturbing, and sometimes avoiding it helps. For instance, rather than waiting until my car is empty of gas, I fill the tank when it's half full, because this costs less than filling the tank when it's almost empty. My reasoning may be imperfect, but the illusion of saving money feels good. The same principle applies to aging. But "feels" is the key word here. I need the same amount of gas no matter when I buy it, and even though I'm not as old as I say I am, this doesn't mean I'm not declining.

So now and then I test myself. I try to evoke the things I forgot in the order in which I forgot them. First it was people's names. We all forget names, probably because when we lived in the trees, although we surely had calls that referred to individuals, we didn't have names as we know them, so we don't have instincts about them. Maybe the brain cells that recognize names and know what to do about them are too few or underdeveloped, so our brain finds names unimportant. It's an unhelpful product of evolution because, in our present condition as civilized people, our name is one of the most important things about us.

Not that our brains care, though. For instance, one day a friend phoned me to ask the name of the man who owns our local bookstore. He's a wonderful person, a pillar of our community whom everyone loves and respects, and I know his name as well as I know my own. But for some reason I couldn't pull it up. I kept trying to force my brain to reveal it, but my brain turned against me. *Get lost*, it said. So I told my friend I'd have to call her back.

The name was somewhere in my head, I knew that, so I tried my method of meditation. I look up at the sky through the trees and the clouds and let it all in. Often enough, this clears my brain of whatever disables it, and sometimes it will address my needs. Not this time, though. For all my brain cared, I'd never met the owner of our bookstore. *Well, fuck you then*, I said to my brain. *I don't even want to know his name.*

My brain answered firmly. *If you're going to be nasty, I'll never tell you*, it said, and I saw there was no hope. Thoroughly humiliated, I had to phone the manager of the bookstore and ask the name of the owner.

"Willard Williams," said the manager instantly, without even having to think. *Yay! Of course! I've known it for years! Everyone knows it! I could have asked anyone! What a good name! What a great name!* I called my friend back and told her.

If our brains won't help us, sometimes these problems can

be solved by others, but not always. The worst one came when I was in that very bookstore waiting to be interviewed about a book I'd written that had just come out. An audience had gathered for the interview, and it was about to start when I noticed my neighbor, a good friend whom I greatly admire. I was thrilled to see him and went over to greet him, but my brain was getting back at me for learning the owner's name without its consent and vengefully whisked my neighbor's name away.

I was helpless. I was horrified. I kept telling my neighbor I was senile and demented. Being the kind, understanding person he is, he didn't feel insulted, but I've seldom been more embarrassed or ashamed. I remember his name as I write this, though, and considering the drama of forgetting it, I'm sure I always will. His name is Kirby.

THE NEXT THING I FORGOT WAS NOUNS. *WHAT'S THE WORD FOR that thing you sweep dust into? It's flat and has a handle? You hold the thing in one hand and a brush in the other?* "Thing" became my favorite word at this point (I use it ninety-five times in this book), but, strangely, for a while I didn't forget verbs, no matter how many nouns I was forgetting. I could even remember unusual verbs such as "slunk" and "retrench." "Slunk" is the past tense of "slink," and although there's some disagreement about how to use "retrench," it means "reduce" or "remove." It's not much of a word, though. I never use it. If I could choose a verb to forget, that verb would be "retrench."

But it wasn't. One day I forgot the verb "to broil." While having dinner with others, I tried to tell them how my husband started kitchen fires when broiling lamb chops, his favorite food, which if I didn't cook on his behalf, he cooked for himself. The first time he set a fire, fire engines arrived with sirens blaring, and the firemen put it out. The same thing happened the second time, but this time the firemen asked my husband why he hadn't cooked some chops for them, because he should have known they'd be coming.

It would have been a nice, quite funny story, but I couldn't remember the verb in question, so I had to describe how the chops were being cooked. "You know, it's when you put something in a pan right under the heater at the top of the oven and turn the heat on high?"

"Broil!" cried the others, but my story was spoiled.

STRANGELY ENOUGH, WORD MEMORY WORKS BOTH WAYS WHEN you're old. When I was a child I learned a little Finnish from my surrogate parents, Tom and Kirsti Johnson. ("Kirsti" sounds Finnish, but "Johnson" doesn't. Tom's family name was Sammallahti, but it was changed to Johnson on Ellis Island by an immigration official who couldn't spell Sammallahti.) Tom and Kirsti did the housekeeping and looked after my brother and me when our parents were out of the house.

One day when I was eighty-five and alone in my kitchen, eating a cookie, I got a surprise. Suddenly, without meaning to, I said *sokeri* out loud. That's a noun, the Finnish word for "sugar," but if an hour earlier you'd asked me for the Finnish word for "sugar," I would have forgotten I knew any Finnish and wouldn't have had a clue. I hadn't willed myself to say it. The word just flew out of my mouth.

Later that day, a song came to mind.

Jaakko kulta, Jaakko kulta,
Herää jo?! Herää jo?
Kello jasi soita, Kello jasi soita,
Pium paum poum, Pium paum poum.

It's the Finnish version of "Frère Jacques," no doubt aroused by *sokeri*. I hadn't been thinking about Tom or Kirsti, and I hadn't heard or thought of that song for at least seventy-five years. But there it was. Nothing like this had ever happened before, and I'm not sure I understand it. Now that my aging brain is resigning, it takes mental experiences that are easy to find, those that it hammered on its wall when it was younger, stronger, and more energetic, and dumps them in a pile on its desk or just drops them somewhere. Among the memories hammered on the wall were words in Finnish, reviving an earlier and perhaps more pleasant time.

Our ancestral primates were not concerned with spelling, which perhaps is why my brain has little interest in that art. I was troubled by the word "aging." These days, it looks to me like "agging," and it bothered me to keep writing it, so for a while I used the British spelling, "ageing." That's much better, but in America it's wrong, so I controlled myself and didn't use it, but not without regret.

As for other words, even if I remember them, I can't think how to spell them, and sometimes I don't even recognize them. I recently didn't recognize the word "laugh" when I saw it, because if you're a bit disoriented, that "augh" part stands out as if it was alone and seems more like "aw" than "aff."

I'm not sure why I'm still able to write. I'm just glad I can. Writing must be in a different part of my brain. In fact, these days my brain seems to think it's always writing, and it makes me edit my thoughts. Not long ago while taking a walk, I saw by the roadside what I thought was a pair of shoes. *A pair of shoes*, my brain said. But my eyes took in more information and pointed out that it wasn't a pair of shoes. My brain reconsidered and said *leaves*, but a moment later changed it to *a pile of leaves*. Don't you see? *A pair of shoes* is "ta tum ta tum," but *leaves* is just "tum." *A pile of leaves* is also "ta tum ta tum"; it matches the earlier statement and would be better in a written sentence. That's some brain I've got here. I just wish it did what I wanted instead of editing unimportant thoughts.

WHEN I WAS YOUNGER, I HAD AMBIENT MEMORY, SO WHEN I'D come in the house and put the car key on the kitchen counter, even if I just dropped it without paying attention, I could mentally retrace my steps and find it. Now that ability is gone.

But I often forget that I've lost my ambient memory, so I still drop important things carelessly, and when I look for them where they belong, they're missing. So now I try to tell myself where I put important things, naming the place out loud so I can hear it.

That's a nice trick, or it is for me, because my brain seems more attracted to the things it hears than to the things it sees. Audio and visual seem to be in different parts of my brain, each focused on its own concerns. Sometimes I leave a note to myself saying where I put something, but then I lose the note, because I wrote it on a little scrap of paper, then forgot what the scrap was for and tossed it in the woodstove. It also helps if I stare at the thing for a minute. *Your flashlight is on the kitchen counter,* I tell myself while staring, and when I want it again, sometimes I can find it.

Because this doesn't always work, forgetting can cause horrors. Not long ago I lost my credit card. It just wasn't there. I wondered if I'd dropped it at the market or left it beside my computer when trying unsuccessfully to buy a book from Amazon. Somehow Amazon thought I wanted to buy two copies of the same book; I couldn't get this corrected, and I knew I had my card when I was trying.

But it wasn't by my computer. Nor had anyone seen it at the market. I felt a sense of panic. What if I'd dropped it outside the market? My mind's eye saw a thief using it to buy a yacht, and I decided to have it stopped, or closed, or canceled, or whatever you say when you don't want someone else to use it.

I didn't have the number of the card, nor did I remember what bank had offered it. At least I knew it was a MasterCard. I found MasterCard's phone number on the internet and called. And what an experience it was. I must have listened to fifty ads before I heard the voice of a real woman.

But her mother tongue wasn't English, so I asked her to speak slowly. She asked what continent I was calling from. Europe? Asia? The Americas? I told her I was calling from the United States. She fussed around for quite a while, then told me her records didn't have my card, but she would call me back in five or ten minutes. At the time, it was five o'clock in the afternoon, so I gave her my phone number and waited. And waited. And no wonder. She was searching through her records for my name, and two of the world's most common names are Elizabeth and Thomas. There must be zillions of us. How would she know which was me?

She phoned me at eleven o'clock when I was fast asleep. I jumped out of bed and answered the phone, and she gave me another number to call because, she said, she'd been too busy to find my records. I tried the number right away and got an irritating buzz. The number was no longer in service.

Maybe I think I don't fear death because sometimes it looks like a solution. By then all I wanted was an end to my problems. Back in bed, I tossed and turned and had bad dreams, probably of someone using my card to buy a mansion, and I woke up telling myself to pull myself together and find a better way to solve the problem.

I took a deep breath. I looked up at the sky. I don't believe in God, but prayer works for some reason, so I said a prayer, remembering my grandmother Nana. Nobody anywhere before or since could find things like she could. Even when she was a hundred years old, her prayer would lead her quickly to whatever anyone had lost.

And then, as often happens, my prayer was answered. I suddenly knew that years ago I'd written down the Master-Card's number, also the phone number to call if I needed to tell MasterCard something. The memory appeared as if it was a photograph. I saw myself writing the numbers with a pen on a midsized piece of paper.

The numbers on the credit card were microscopic or, to put it more accurately, they seemed small to someone whose eyes were eighty-seven years old. I saw myself using a magnifying glass to read them. But my mental photo didn't show what I'd done with the piece of paper. I thought it must be in the house, so I searched. And searched. For hours, I searched. And yes, I found it in one of my hundreds of files, not arranged in any order, and this one was marked "Credit Cards." Not only had I written the card number, I'd written the expiration date, also the little numerical password on the back, and also the number to call.

How's that for organization? And I'd thought I was senile. I called that number, got an instant answer from a real person, and canceled the card with the promise of a new one in two days. I then lived happily ever after. Or reasonably happily ever after. Or reasonably happily for a while.

But things got even better. I called my daughter in Texas to share this experience, and she told me that if your credit card is stolen and used by someone else, you're not held responsible. She didn't have to pay the $5,000 a thief had charged on her card, an amount she noticed when she got the bill. While I was suffering, I didn't know that you're not responsible for illegal charges (or perhaps I knew but had forgotten), but I know now, and because the experience was so intense, I'll probably remember, so this makes me even happier.

Never mind that the whole thing was a mistake, and I wouldn't be charged for illegal purchases. I'd made a note with the card number and all the other information, I'd put it in a file marked "Credit Cards," and when I needed it, I pulled it out. Disregard the first part of my story, accept the last part, and you'll see that I'm functioning beautifully.

THE CREDIT-CARD EXPERIENCE ENDED HAPPILY, BUT MANY DON'T, and at one point I wondered how much time I waste looking for lost items. It takes me at least fifteen or twenty minutes to find one, often longer, which means that since I became forgetful, I waste more than ten hours each month, which means that I've spent at least three months of my life doing nothing but searching. In that amount of time I could have gone on a vacation. But what choice did I have? I must find my things! I wish I hadn't learned how much time I was wasting.

I don't like to waste time, because my sense of it has changed. I wake up before sunrise and soon enough it's dark again. I start work on Monday and suddenly it's Sunday—a whole week gone! Most people like Fridays better than Mondays, but I like Mondays better than Fridays, because Friday means that a week has gone and I wonder what happened.

The world has changed. That's what happened. Nothing is the same as it was when I was young, and people do things differently. For this they must use new technology, but that's beyond my powers. My son gave me a thing that makes phone calls, calculates, predicts the weather, gives driving directions, and also does more things I don't know about, but I couldn't figure out how to use it. He tried to teach me, but I couldn't remember what he said, so I got myself a simple little cell phone that just makes phone calls, and I wear it on a string around my neck or leave it on the floor when I'm taking a shower. Then I can call 911 if I fall and can't get up. And this could happen, because taking a shower makes me light-headed, which is sometimes a sign of a stroke.

I use a computer as if it was a typewriter. That's an old-fashioned device something like a computer keyboard, each letter with its own key, which, when you hit it with your finger, puts the letter on a piece of paper. These days, the world runs on the internet, so I also use the computer for email, but often enough I do something wrong and make a big mess, which takes hours of fixing.

Even so, I use my computer for writing because it's faster than handwriting, which of course is how most of us wrote even after typewriters were invented. The quality of what you write isn't as good if you use a computer, but the writing goes faster.

Even so, my computer has a mind of its own and thinks it knows more than I do, so sometimes it changes things automatically, and my time is wasted trying to fix them. Fortunately, I'm the client of a company with wonderful people who will log onto my computer and solve the problems. I try to watch how they do it, so I'll be able to do it myself, but the processes are complicated and whoever is doing them does them quickly, so it all seems too difficult and I don't learn.

Then I remember my grandmother Nana, who was born during the Civil War. She was afraid of the telephone. At times she'd be the only grown-up in the house when the phone rang, and she'd steel herself to pick up the receiver. She'd shout, "MISSUS! . . . MARSHALL! . . . IS! . . . NOT! . . . HOME!" and hang up forcefully. Mrs. Marshall was my mother, but Nana's name was also Mrs. Marshall. However, she must have been in her seventies when phones became common, so she never imagined that a call would be for her.

But sometimes it was. When I was in my teens, I called our house from a neighbor's house because our door was locked,

Nana didn't like to answer the door, and I didn't have a key. The phone rang a long time, and when I heard her starting to shout, "Missus . . . Marshall . . . ," I screamed, "Nana! Nana! It's me!" But she was hard of hearing, just as I am now, and she banged the receiver down as usual. I think of her when I fail to understand my cell phone or computer, which is often.

SO I'LL TAKE A DEEP BREATH AND REMEMBER THE GOOD OLD DAYS when life was easy, when I could remember where things were and knew how to use them. I live in the country house my father built for us in 1935, and in the kitchen is a second-hand woodstove made in the 1800s. The stove works as well as it did on the day it was made, and its functions are intuitive. You don't need to learn how it works. If you look at it, you can see how it works, and you already know that if you put wood and paper in it and drop a match on the paper, the wood will eventually burn.

That stove is better than most items made today, even if it doesn't have as many options. All it does is warm the house and let you cook on it. But I don't need lots of options. I keep as close as I can to familiar items like my woodstove, which I know.

It's soothing. I still have the washboard we used to scrub the laundry before washing machines were invented, also the clothespins with which we hung the laundry on the clothesline outside. I keep the washboard just to look at—now I do the laundry in a washing machine. Sometimes I hang the laundry on the clothesline with the clothespins, but more often I put it in the dryer.

Sometimes I call my refrigerator the "icebox" from the days when we got ice from a pond, kept it covered in a shed, and brought pieces of it to the house when we needed them. If others are looking for milk and I say, "There's some in the icebox," most elders won't notice, but young people look at me strangely.

Things move too fast. My son's family now has a little round Google thing the size and shape of a doughnut, but without a hole in the middle, that answers questions for you. No doubt it can also hear you talking in the room and if so is undoubtedly transferring your remarks to Google, so I think it's best to be in another room if you say you're going to cheat on your income taxes or drive when your voice sounds like you're drunk. In short, the Google thing is weird. I look at my landline phone and at the *Encyclopedia Britannica* that's on a shelf beside it and say, *Enough already*.

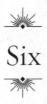

Six

Hopefully, I've explained the flaws of unfamiliar things. Now I should look at myself as if I was a thing. Am I doing as well as my woodstove? Probably not, although it seemed worth finding out, but when I did, I got discouraged. Old people are set in their ways and tend to keep making the same mistakes. I'd discouraged myself by learning how much time I wasted looking for things, but that didn't stop me from testing my heart to learn how often it beat.

I went to my modern kitchen stove. It's close to my woodstove, but it's electric and has a timer. I put my left front fingers on the inside of my right wrist. There, I located an artery or a capillary—whatever—and felt the little bumps as my blood pushed through it, thanks to the repeated beating of my heart. After setting the timer for one minute, I began to count. My heart beat eighty times—yes, eighty times; that's more than once a second—before the buzzer sounded. Wow!

My husband could do math in his head, but he was no longer living. I do math on my fingers, but all I have are ten. I spent the next twenty minutes finding our little calculator to learn how many times my heart would beat in a day, and— wow again—it beats 4,800 times in an hour, which, when multiplied by 24, means it beats 115,200 times each day.

I multiplied this by 365 and found a number almost too big to read—my heart beats 42,048,000 times in a year. This means that on the day I took the measurement, my heart has pumped steadily day and night 3,668,774,400 times since I was born. The actual number is even higher, because my heart began beating while I was a fetus, and it's been beating since I took the measurement.

This gives you respect for the human heart, especially since the heart does this day after day, year after year, never resting even for a moment, pushing oxygen and nutrients around your body with your blood, bringing the carbon dioxide you've rejected to your lungs so you can blow it out and the wet waste to your bladder so you can pee it out. My heart knows that if it stops, the rest of this will also stop, and we will be in that grave on the north side of the hill. But even so, to pump without resting for eighty-seven years is quite an achievement. Few machines that are made today will boast of such a record. I felt a little proud of my heart.

BUT AFTER I THOUGHT ABOUT IT FOR A WHILE, THAT LAST NUMBER seemed like a lot. My heart can't do that forever, and I kind of wished I didn't know the number. My unconscious mind, where my instincts hide, produced an image of the Grim Reaper.

So I turned my attention to my other body parts, and here I didn't need to measure anything—I have daily reminders of failure. I've recently noticed that I'm sometimes light-headed, and I don't know what this means. The skin of my scalp sometimes tingles as if my head is preparing to fly off, so one day I looked up the symptom on the internet and didn't like what I saw. I'd found a site that listed seven reasons, the first of which said I was having a stroke, which bothered me so much that I stopped reading and didn't see the other six reasons.

But I did change the way I took a shower. Now, instead of standing up straight, I lean back against the shower wall, so if I have a stroke I'll slide down to a sitting position instead of falling forward and smashing my forehead on the shower's tile floor. I also put my little cell phone on the inside edge of the shower where I'll be able to reach it. With this in mind, I reconsider an interesting book I read on this subject, *Old Age:*

The Best Age, by Abram T. Collier, and I'm not so sure about that word "best." Maybe the title should be *Old Age Is Okay If You Can Handle the Problems.*

I'M LOSING MY STRENGTH. I ONCE COULD LIFT 100 POUNDS WITH no problem. I could lift even more. I could lift my husband—he weighed 160 pounds—if I surprised him by grabbing him around the waist from behind, heaving him up, and spinning him around, although he didn't like me to do this. But since I've grown old, everything else has grown heavy. What once felt like 20 pounds now feels like 80 pounds. I hesitate before lifting something that weighs 10 pounds, because I wonder how much it will strain me.

I used to carry big loads of . . . what do you call those things? Logs? Sticks? They're pieces of trees I keep in the basement and burn in the abovementioned woodstove. Now I carry them two at a time, which helps with the weight but which I do at some risk, because the staircase to the basement is dark even with the light on and the stairs are uneven. I risk a bad fall when I go up or down them, which I do every time I get wood.*

What's more, I'm shrinking. I was five foot two, but somehow I lost two inches. Do men also shrink? I don't know any

---

* Aha! Now I remember the word for what I carry up the cellar stairs. The word is "firewood."

men who seem to be shrinking, although I'm told they do, but I know women who are shrinking, some more than me, and if I shrink any more, many things in my house will be unreachable.

That's the downside, but even so there's something marvelous about shrinking. You might think that as you became shorter, you would also become wider, because your mass should be the same. But this doesn't happen. As you become smaller you retain the same appearance. Most of you seems to shrink at the same time in the same way, no matter how many inches you lose. I can't imagine how we do this.

The strange thing is that your teeth don't shrink. I find that my teeth, once touching very lightly, are now squeezed together more tightly, so when I eat something with fibers like lettuce or cabbage, I find some of my molars stuck with vegetable strands and in need of careful flossing.

Oh, well. Do tight teeth and size loss matter all that much except that dental hygiene takes longer, you can't reach as high as you once could, and your clothes are too big? My jeans used to be the same length as my legs and came smoothly to my ankles, and now they come crumpled to my ankles because my legs must be shorter. But so what?

What matters is that my bones are deteriorating. I learned this one night while walking down a dark hallway, tripping on a dog, and falling sideways. The dog wasn't hurt, but even though I didn't land hard, my hip broke, which meant my bones needed improvement, or at least should keep what strength they have, so once a month I take a bone-strengthening pill. But time flies when you're old, and a month goes by so fast that sometimes I don't take the pill because I think I just took one.

A surgeon fixed the broken hip. He told me he had nailed the broken parts together. Yes, he said "nailed," and he meant it. I see myself unconscious on the operating table while he hammers a nail into one of my bones, and I wonder if the hammering caused damage. Since then I've suffered from restless legs that surprise me by kicking for no reason, a real nuisance when I'm trying to sleep. Fortunately, pills exist that help this.

I'M SUPPOSED TO PUT DROPS IN MY EYES. IF I OCCASIONALLY FORGET the bone-strengthening pill I'm forced to swallow every month, I never forget the eye drops, because I'm getting glaucoma. This causes loss of peripheral vision and lots of other problems, and without these eye drops I'd be almost blind. I may go blind anyway, but not quickly, although I learned of a woman who had glaucoma and woke up one morning to find that she was totally blind. I'm sure that was terrible for her, and would be terrible for me, especially since I'm the only human in my house and can't find things even with my now moderate eyesight. I'll avoid being blind for as long as I can.

My hearing is another matter, and it too is failing. I learned that hearing loss and Alzheimer's are sometimes connected, which seems like bad news. Are the mistakes I make due to carelessness or is Alzheimer's approaching? We're told that symptoms of this dreadful condition are loss of bladder and bowel control, also groaning, grunting, and moaning. I still control my bowels, thank goodness, and except for occasional little leaks when I'm coughing or hear water running I don't wet my pants, and although sometimes I groan, I seldom grunt and never moan, so I'm hopeful.

IF MY FAVORITE WORD IS "THING," FOR MANY YEARS MY SECOND-favorite word was "what." I learned this when an audiologist said, "Are you experiencing hearing loss?" and I said, "What?" My question suggested that I was experiencing hearing loss, and although I can't remember the word for that particular condition, it has to do with certain sounds and tones my ears no longer recognize. Those of us with this condition can hear people speaking, but we catch only part of what they're saying. If we want to know what we're missing, we must ask them to repeat themselves while we cup our hands behind our ears and lean toward them.

The audiologist advised me to buy a hearing aid. When I asked about the price, she said that mine would cost $3,000. That seemed prohibitive, but imagine my surprise when I learned that it's just for one ear. You pay $6,000 if you want to hear with both ears. Medicare doesn't cover this, and I don't spend that kind of money on myself, so I decided to stay with "What?"

BUT WORRY PURSUED ME. WHAT ABOUT MY BRAIN? I'D LEARNED that we don't hear with our ears; we hear with our brains, which process electric signals that our eardrums catch and carry inside. This means that our ears are something like our eyes, two round balls that are parts of our brains and stick out through our faces to catch visual signals. Our ears are two cups that stick out of our heads to bring sounds through the eardrums to cells in the brain that determine what they mean. The cells can store the meaning for a while, but cells replace themselves, and if your hearing declines for several years, the cells that knew what a sound meant have been replaced by cells that don't. This is bad for your brain and is believed to contribute to dementia.

I WAS TOLD THAT BABIES CRY RIGHT AFTER THEY'RE BORN BEcause their brain cells are uneducated. Suddenly their newborn brains get a tsunami of signals—sight, sound, smell, touch, and who knows what else. The baby's inexperienced brain knows nothing. The poor little thing can't make out what's happening and doesn't know how to handle this, and the only way to communicate distress is by crying.

The problem applies in reverse when you're old. Let's say

you hear tree frogs. They're singing, but not as loudly as they used to. You almost can't hear them, and you imagine they're farther away than they used to be.

Actually your hearing is failing. A year or two later you don't hear them at all, and you assume they've disappeared for some reason. What really happened is that your cells that understood the song were replaced by cells that weren't receiving the information, and this has diminished your brain. My brain must be diminishing, and as is true of many problems, the longer we wait to solve them, the worse they get. I decided to stop saying "What?"

BUT RATHER THAN DISHING OUT $6,000 FOR HEARING AIDS, I thought it best to shop around and found several kinds of hearing aids at substantially lower prices. The least expensive were about $40 for one ear or $80 for two ears, and others cost from $100 to $500—that's $200 to $1,000 if you want to hear with both ears. You can buy them on the internet or in in big-box stores like Walmart, but you take what you get. Because hearing loss has several forms, not everyone's ears are the same, so I decided to shop for audiologists.

When making the necessary appointments, I found (at least in my area of New Hampshire) that hearing aids offered by most professional audiologists cost about the same—$3,000 per ear. That's the bad news. The good news is that a responsible audiologist tests your ears to determine your form of hearing loss, and the hearing aids are guaranteed to work. Two of the audiologists told me I could try the aids for several months, and if they didn't fit my needs, I could return them for a full refund, no questions asked.

At each office I visited, an audiologist tested my ears and then fitted them with aids that suited my hearing condition. On each visit, we went outside to try them. When I visited the first audiologist, I heard a bird's high-pitched song. Wow! I hadn't heard anything like that for quite a while. At least I knew what it was. Then the audiologist asked me a question, speaking in his normal voice. I heard him perfectly, even when he was thirty feet away. So until I answered him, the hearing aids seemed great.

But when I answered, I heard a bellowing voice I didn't recognize. If I hadn't been able to feel myself speaking, I wouldn't have dreamed it was me. Then a truck drove by. It sounded like overhead thunder. The audiologist's office was next to a highway, and the traffic, moving at fifty miles an hour, made a deafening roar. I heard my unfamiliar voice complain about the noise. "You get used to it," I heard the audiologist saying.

But what if I didn't? I decided to do more shopping, and thanks to another audiologist I found hearing aids that softened the loud sounds. With these aids, the traffic sounded normal, perhaps normally noisy but not roaring. My voice still seemed strange, but at least the volume was normal.

Not only that, but when I had my first appointment with this audiologist, he sent me away and gave me another appointment, telling me to have my ears cleared of wax so he could examine my eardrums.

That seemed both useful and essential. Other audiologists hadn't asked for this, so I was impressed. Also, the hearing aids this audiologist suggested fit better and were less visible than any I'd tried before. I was surprised they were so small and inconspicuous, but more surprised when the audiologist told me he had hearing aids like them, and even more surprised when he pulled one off his ear to show me he was wearing them. I'd been looking at his face for twenty minutes and hadn't noticed. That was nice, as was the natural quality of the sounds. This was good enough for me. I bought them.

Hearing aids run on electricity. Some have batteries so tiny that they're almost microscopic. If your eyes are good enough to see these little batteries, you replace them once a month, being careful not to drop one, because if you do, you'll have to get down on your arthritic knees to try to find it. The tiny thing is round and lightweight, so it rolls away quickly. It could be in the dark space under your sofa before it occurs to you to look there. You'll have to sweep your hands over the floor under the sofa, and even then the battery is so small you might not feel it, or it's against the wall behind the sofa where you can't reach it, assuming it's really there. With luck, a friend or relative will help you. She'll come with a flashlight and spend the next half hour searching. Just hope it isn't on the open floor and one of you steps on it.

Other hearing aids get their power from a charger, and

depending on the model the charge lasts two days and a night. Chargers are also expensive, but the hearing aids I chose came with a charger. So I was happy to think that my wobbling brain would be somewhat protected, I would understand most of what everyone says, even in a noisy restaurant, and I wouldn't shout "What?" anymore. The irony is that despite a generous discount, the hearing aids cost so much that I can't afford to go to a restaurant. Months or even years may pass before I buy anything at all.

WAS IT WORTH IT? I DOUBT THAT ANYTHING I EVER BOUGHT BE-fore has been so worth it. The first day I wore them, I heard not only what people were saying but also such things as a clock ticking, the wind in the trees, and a dog barking far away. These sounds as such aren't important or impressive. Nothing would change if you didn't hear them. But to me they were extremely important. For the first time in years, I felt joined to my world.

You see what's in front of you, but sound is all around you. Suddenly you're part of your environment—right inside it, not just looking at it. My hearing loss had come so gradually I hadn't realized what I was missing. And then, like a miracle, my environment was no longer like a photo—it was living and breathing all around me. I felt like I felt when I was forty, the only difference being that when I was forty, I never imagined my hearing would fail.

It's also nice to hear everything that someone else is saying, not just snatches of it. The more of our hearing we lose, the less we tend to socialize, if only because others don't hurry to socialize with us except out of pity. They tire of our shouting "What?" and it's hard for them to carry on a conversation when they must keep repeating themselves. They'll talk for a while to the face that looks intensely at them, but soon they'll realize they're not understood and they'll turn to talk with someone else.

Most of us don't shout "What?" and I don't either, or not as often as I'm saying. Most of us just sit there smiling, pretending we're hearing what everyone says. Even so, others notice. We may not laugh when someone says something funny until we realize that others are laughing. So we just sit there looking dull until we realize we should be laughing, and then when we laugh suddenly, someone is sure to notice. Those who realize you're not hearing them may feel a little offish. Will they invite you the next time?

The less we socialize, the more alone and abandoned we feel. If we don't hear well, we can't reach out, so we stay inside ourselves. That's why I offer my story about the hearing-aid experience, hoping that some of my readers with hearing loss might consider the purchase of hearing aids before their brains get damaged.

One friend bought hearing aids from a big department store (I don't know which one) that seemed to be as good as mine but cost much less, and another friend bought hearing aids on the internet. These were even less expensive (although I don't know how much), and she's happy with them. She also was lucky, and the reason I didn't do what she did was that when it comes to machinelike objects such as hearing aids, I'm often unlucky.

For others who feel cautious, it may be worth it to be tested by a professional audiologist who will identify and measure your hearing loss and offer hearing aids guaranteed to help you. Anyway, that's what I did. The price covered not only a charger, but also unlimited visits to the audiologist and all kinds of warranties and adjustments—even if I lose a hearing aid or step on one, it will be replaced for free—so I'm content.

Seven

I n the past when I'd think about something, I'd think in words, as if I were speaking to myself. I'd be walking to my office and my mind would ask in English, *Did you tun off the light in the hall?* So I'd go back to look. But now that I'm old, my brain prefers visual messages. More often than not, my mind's eye sees the light on in the hall, and without my brain verbalizing about it, I go back to look.

Important studies suggest with good reason that animals remember in pictures as well as in odors and sounds. To me this seems obvious. It's been proved that many animals (chickens and certain fish, to mention but two) are better at recognizing human individuals than we humans are, retaining the image of that human even if they've only seen the human once. Some of these animals can even recognize the human from a photograph. Thus it's hard to imagine that they don't apply this skill to other objects and events. You see something, you store the image, and flash it up when the occasion demands.

As we age, the present falls away and we revitalize the past. Many elderly people will tell you they remember things from the past better than things from the present. My memory took photos of hundreds of things from my childhood, but in the present I must think pretty hard before I remember what I did this afternoon.

My memory photos from the distant past aren't of unusual things, nor did they seem unusual at the time. I see a mental photo of my little brother climbing in front of me to the top shelf of the linen closet. This was our den when we pretended we were raccoons. I see our mother's mother, Gran, pointing us out to our mother, saying we would mess up the linen in the closet. I see our mother thinking it over and deciding to leave us alone. It wasn't an important moment, just a random childhood memory, but it's as clear in my mind as if it had happened today.

My mind reviews scenes that range from the linen closet to the sight of my daughter lying injured on the road. What's interesting to me, if not comfortable, is that although my childhood memories are relatively neutral, my midlife memories tend to be sad or even tragic. My daughter was injured in a tractor accident forty-four years ago, when I was forty-two and she was seventeen.

Her back was broken in the accident so she was paralyzed from the waist down, but she made an enviable life for herself. She worked for the rights of disabled people, taking part in hundreds of massive demonstrations for which she was arrested at least thirty times and put in jail. She testified before Congress about disability issues, she was one of the people whose work produced the Americans with Disabilities Act, and she was invited to the White House by President George H. W. Bush to see him sign it into law. So when I think of her life, I feel happiness and pride. But my brain shows her lying on the road.

I think of Pearl, my beloved Australian shepherd, and several pictures appear. Some are positive, but mostly I see her looking at me with a loving, trusting expression while a veterinarian gives her a lethal injection because of incurable cancer. This image comes up all the time.

I see my husband as he was dying, my father as he was dying, and my mother as she was dying as clearly as if I were looking at them now, and I wonder what these visual messages are for. Surely we're programmed to keep them. It seems safe to say that other animals have similar images and also are programmed to keep them. Why are we inclined to keep the sad things and mentally view them often? Perhaps we do it for an ancient reason. Perhaps our unconscious minds are saying, *Look at what happened. Take care of your own.*

I'd say that our visual memories could be the most important memories. In my case, many of them would be memories of learning about the natural world. My dad would take me and my brother into the woods, where we'd find the tracks of animals and learn the names of trees. My memories are pictures of the tracks and the trees—I still see a line of fox tracks on a dusty trail and the tracks of a very large cat in the snow near our swamp. I remember the large tracks as if I were looking at them now—they could have been those of a Canada lynx or a mountain lion who allegedly lived in our area.

I've always been fascinated by the big cats, and one of the brightest, most complete pictures that arises is that of a lion in the Kalahari. This picture is more like a video. My brother and I were far out in the veld, walking along, unarmed of course, because we did as the San did, and they didn't carry weapons except when they were hunting. We came around some bushes and found ourselves face-to-face with a lion who was standing about twenty feet away. We froze.

He watched us politely. We remained frozen. Helpfully, the San had told us never to turn and run because the lion will chase you and can run much faster, but instead to assume an indifferent expression and walk away at an oblique angle. But we were riveted. We just stood there staring while the lion watched us with mild interest. Then he assumed an indifferent expression and walked away at an oblique angle. Evidently there was agreement about what best to do.

I can relive this interesting experience whenever I like. It begins as we come around the bushes and ends with us watching the hindquarters of the lion as he walks away, his tail held low but twitching slowly as if our presence or behavior had annoyed him slightly.

He also showed us what the San considered an oblique angle. If you imagine your watch with yourself at six o'clock, you should imagine the lion walking away at a natural pace toward two-thirty.

Most such memories are designed to help us. This one is no longer useful, as I may never meet a lion in New Hampshire, but it's exciting and fun, and like many other memories from the past, I like to call it up from time to time for no reason other than I like it.

Eight

You begin to age when you're fifty and you think you're getting old. If really old people hear you say this, assuming they can hear you and have enough cognition to understand what you said, they scoff. They snort. They say, "Just you wait."

Real aging starts when your oldest child is fifty. You are in your seventies, you call your children "kids," and realize how young you were when you were in your fifties. Down go your hearing, your eyesight, and your memory. You're seen as different. You don't matter. You're a burden to society. While President Trump was giving a king's ransom in tax cuts to the richest 1 percent of our population, he cut the funding for

Meals on Wheels. He didn't worry that old people might go hungry—he knew if they were starved, they'd be too weak to get to the polls and vote for his opponent.

Old age has its physical problems, but it has social problems too. Our culture divides us into groups according to our age; each group is treated differently, and we pass into them slowly. The best description of the passage I've ever seen was in an email from my good friend, the poet Howard Nelson. "Heading off canoe camping today," he wrote, "with 2 kids (45 & 49 years old) & 3 grandkids. Am I the leader of this expedition? I think at this point I am transitioning into the old guy they take along."

OUR AGE GROUPS RESEMBLE THOSE OF THE SAN. BOTH CULTURES recognize four. No doubt most cultures do. Group One is babies. Group Two is children, which you join when you can speak a full sentence and run fast, not just toddle. Group Three is grown-ups, which you join when you're full-grown and have finished or are finishing your education. And Group Four is old people. The important difference between us and the San is that the San respected the old people.

When the San lived as hunter-gatherers, old people were essential. They had information from their own past, and they remembered the information their elders had provided from their past, so the chain of memory from both generations could go back for more than a century. This had value, because in the case of certain bad things that happened rarely (such as serious droughts), old people remembered how they or their elders managed and could provide the information.

The San respected the elderly very deeply. The word *N!a'an* (which means "old") was something like a title, such as Sir, Lord, or Admiral, but came after the name, not before. If lions appeared by night at an encampment, some of the men would take burning branches from their fires and shake them at the lions while saying politely, "Old lions, we respect you, but this is our place. We ask you to leave." The lions would look at the men, think about it briefly, and then, because they'd been treated with respect as if they were elders, they'd turn politely and walk away.

But in the case of the San as well as in our case, the elders didn't contribute much more than helpful memories; in our case, we have written records of past events and don't need our elders to remember them for us. Our society respects old people only if they're famous, and often not even then. The rest of us just spend taxpayers' money to keep ourselves alive, and most people seem to dislike us, old women more than old men. Consider the countless so-called jokes found on countless internet sources about demented old women who wet their pants.

As for general disrespect, I'm speaking of our social values, not our family values. Our families and friends continue to value us, and if they're younger than we are, they comfort us. I once told a good friend that I wasn't the sharpest tool in the shed, and she said, "You always were and always will be the sharpest tool in the shed."

I'd said I wasn't the sharpest tool while fumbling through my pockets in search of my wallet, which I feared I'd forgotten to bring—we had just had lunch at a restaurant at my invitation, and I wanted to pay the bill—so my friend's kind remark was far from true, but it made me unreasonably happy. (My wallet was in the left rear pocket of my jeans. I paid the bill.)

Another friend told me I was beautiful. My skin is wrinkled and covered with dark blotches, my thinning hair is white with gray patches, my eyebrows are too, my waistline is bigger than my hipline, and I have only one breast and no uterus (I was spayed when I was in my forties), so I wouldn't do well in the Miss America contest. But again I was unreasonably happy.

Those two events reflect our personal values. Our social values are not the same, partly because the elderly are financial burdens. Take me, for instance. I have Medicare and Social Security plus a veteran's benefit from the VA, because I'm the widow of a veteran who served during wartime and died of ALS—that's amyotrophic lateral sclerosis, or Lou Gehrig's disease—which is considered to be service related no matter when it starts.

That's a nice chunk of money every month. The taxes I paid throughout my life were meant to provide for these payments, but today's taxpayers may need to cover medical payments beyond what my taxes have provided and could arise before I'm gone. Thus we elders don't add much to society, and we cost a lot of money. No wonder we're devalued.

Group Two (children) also costs money, because children need schools. But children grow up and contribute. Our Group Four (elders) contributes relatively little and goes on costing more. At the time of this writing, President Trump and his followers want to privatize Medicare and Social Security, dismantle Obamacare, and allow the exclusion of people with preexisting conditions. This will leave many people out in the cold, as many of us, especially the elderly, have at least one preexisting condition, often more.

The most honored group is Group Three, the grown-ups. These are the vital, functional people who have jobs, who run the country, who get things done and keep everything going. This group is wide ranging, extending from people in their twenties to those in their sixties or seventies, as long as those in the latter group don't match our cultural picture of "old." Group Three has the important people. We stay there as long as we can.

Group Three grown-ups see one another as more or less the same; thus no one seems to notice much difference between people at the near end and those at the far end. When I was in my twenties one of my best friends was Niña Coveney, a wonderful woman in her sixties, and when I was in my sixties one of my closest friends was and still is Sy Montgomery, who was in her twenties when we met. Niña is no longer living, but my relationship with Sy continues unchanged.

Despite the difference in our ages, we're soul mates. This began the day we met. Sy had a ferret, and when I reached into his cage, he bit my finger. Sy was impressed with my indifference—I wiped the blood off on my jeans and went on talking—and our friendship grew from there.

When Sy was in India with National Geographic for a film about man-eating tigers, she came upon a tiger's turd in the forest and brought it all the way back to the United States and through customs, so she could give it to me as a Christmas present. The tiger had eaten a langur monkey, and the langur's hairs stuck out of the turd.

Never had I received a more important present. Sy tells me I'd ask people if they wanted to see a langur monkey after he's been through the intestines of a tiger. I don't believe that anyone did. This was in 1993, and twenty-six years later that turd, wrapped up, is still in my freezer. Now Sy is in her sixties and has a good friend in his thirties. The important feature in this context is that at the times we met, we were all in Group Three despite our ages.

So reaching Group Four can be interesting. Until then, a large percentage of the people you know don't know or care how old you are, and you don't know or care how old they are, because your ages aren't important. Not long ago I was talking with a nice man I had known since the 1960s and told him I was writing a book about aging. He asked how old I was, and I said I was eighty-seven. He was shocked. He was in his early seventies, not quite in Group Four. I was shocked too. Both of us suddenly saw there was a huge age gap between us, something neither of us had noticed for al-most sixty years.

IF YOU'RE STRONGLY TIED TO YOUNGER UNRELATED PEOPLE, those people won't change the way they see you. We don't dis-credit friends or family members just because they're old. But others may not be so forgiving, as I first learned when outside our local market. A woman I knew came out of the store, and while we were standing on the sidewalk chatting about other people, she told me of a woman in her seventies who was look-ing for a retirement community. Seventies didn't seem old to me, so I said I wouldn't be ready to do that and I would soon be eighty.

My friend was speechless. She suddenly realized that I was old and she'd taken me for a Group Three grown-up. She said I didn't look almost eighty. I had gray hair and wrinkles, so I wasn't sure what I was missing, and I felt a little guilty, as if I'd been trying to deceive her.

MY NEXT SUCH EXPERIENCE TOOK PLACE IN A RESTAURANT where I often went with my son's family. They live across the road from me and often invite me for dinner, and because I've forgotten how to cook, I reciprocate by taking them to the res-taurant. The owner knew us and would come to our table to

ELIZABETH MARSHALL THOMAS

talk. But for some reason we stopped going to restaurants, and several months passed before we went to that restaurant again.

When at last we did, the owner came to our table as always, glad to see us. He greeted my son, who was across the table from me, and then he greeted my grandson on my left. But when his gaze fell on me, it paused for a nanosecond and passed to my son's wife on my right. I started to say something, but he didn't seem to hear me. It had been months since he'd seen me, and he had a fresh look at me. He saw an old woman, and for him she wasn't there.

We still go to that restaurant, and he always greets my family members, but ever since then he's ignored me. Because no scandals surround me as far as I know—I've never done anything wrong in that restaurant like shouting "Horrible food!" and throwing it on the floor, and I've always been polite and friendly, never failing to leave a 20 percent tip—I can only assume that he doesn't acknowledge me because while seeing me often, he didn't notice my age, and when he noticed, he erased me.

I once asked him why he never spoke to me. The question didn't seem to surprise him, and whatever he said, he didn't deny it. But I missed most of his answer because I couldn't quite hear it, and not wanting to increase his displeasure with me, I didn't ask again. This was before I had hearing aids.

I'M NOT THE ONLY ONE WHO GETS IGNORED. ONCE I WAS SITTING in a waiting room used by several doctors and got into a con-

84

versation with the elderly woman beside me. She told me about gardening, which was her hobby, and I told her I'd heard that the doctor she was about to see was also a gardener. "You must have lots to talk about," I said.

"To him I'm the obese diabetic," she said. "He doesn't even say hello when he sees me. We don't talk about anything." After a moment she added, "I'm here on referral," which I believe she said to suggest that this doctor wasn't her choice and her regular doctor was nicer.

It seems that many doctors see their elderly patients as a case of this or a case of that and have no other interest in us, which is probably okay if the doctors treat the conditions that bring us to them. But some doctors don't even do that. After my husband was diagnosed with ALS, he was hospitalized because, along with ALS, he had pneumonia. The hospital doctor came to his room, took one look at him, and wrote in his report that my husband was a spinal cord–injured paraplegic with an indwelling catheter. A catheter can lead to bladder infections, so the doctor prescribed an overpowering antibiotic to be taken by a continuous intravenous injection delivered from a large apparatus on wheels.

My husband wasn't a paraplegic and didn't have an indwelling catheter, which the doctor could have learned, either by asking him or by lifting the sheet that covered him. That would have taken less than a second, but why bother? My husband was old and sick and would die soon anyway. Who cared about his condition?

I cared, and so did a nurse I'll call Wanda. She was his

caregiver at home and would visit him at the hospital, and she was in the room when someone delivered the doctor's report. It was given to her, and when I arrived, she gave it to me. Both of us were amazed by it. I said I'd report its mistakes, and I did.

But when Wanda's boss learned she had given an erroneous report to the patient's wife, thus exposing a hospital doctor, she called Wanda to her office to berate and threaten her. The hospital might take revenge by not recommending their caregiving service, she said, and to our dismay she removed Wanda as my husband's case manager. When my husband came home, a different nurse arrived to help him. At the time, we didn't know why.

Wanda knew she'd endangered her job by giving me the report, but she did it anyway. Patients and their families are entitled to their medical reports, and we were grateful. But I wondered about the woman who rebuked her. It mattered nothing to this woman that my husband, already vulnerable and seriously compromised, might be more seriously compromised by a continuous dose of a powerful antibiotic he didn't need.

Faced with the doctor's garbled report and the giant apparatus that by then was attached to my husband, I called his lifelong doctor, Victor Gurewich, who taught at Harvard Medical School. He and my husband had known each other since Victor graduated from that school with an MD.

My husband had been given a urine test. Victor asked to see it. He found no bladder infection and told us to remove the apparatus immediately. We did and sent it back, surprising the company that owned it, and my husband was okay for years thereafter. I should add that we were in New Hampshire and Victor was seventy miles away in Massachusetts, or we would have gone to him in the first place. To him, my husband was an interesting, knowledgeable friend who was well worth fixing. That's how Victor saw his patients.

SINCE THEN I'VE LEARNED THAT MANY DOCTORS SHY AWAY FROM old sick people because doctors want to cure, and the wreckage of an old person with an incurable condition is something they'd rather avoid. That's why many doctors don't like us, no matter how much business we bring them.

Studies show that increasingly fewer doctors specialize in geriatrics, because the ideal patient for a doctor is a young person with one medical problem. That person can be fixed. An old person with diabetes, ALS, or weakening bones and memory problems—in other words someone who has nothing curable and will die soon anyway—seems like garbage to many doctors, or perhaps is too much of a challenge. Thus an old person is best seen as a condition—the ALS case, the obese diabetic—not as a highly educated person who lived on three continents and speaks six languages, not as a successful, capable gardener who understands botany, not as a functioning human like themselves.

NOT LONG AGO I NOTICED THAT MY HEART STOPPED BEATING. This was temporary, but to play it safe, my son brought me to the emergency room of that hospital. At the time, we were afraid the ER doctor might be the one who assumed my husband had an indwelling catheter, but that doctor was gone (I hope he was fired), and the new doctor was a friend of my son's. When he came into the room where we were waiting, the two men hailed each other joyously, throwing their arms around each other and turning their backs to me. They laughed and talked, catching up on what they'd been doing, until the doctor shook my son's hand with enthusiasm, clapped him on the back, said they must have dinner together soon, and left the room.

After that, he must have spoken to the people at the desk, because later someone came to stick a little gizmo on my chest that would monitor my heartbeat. I was told to wear it for two weeks, so I did, and the gizmo showed that I was fine.

This means our mission to the ER was more or less successful, but it would have been nice if the doctor had spoken, if only once, to that elderly woman in the room who seemed to have the heart problem.

By now I've identified several doctors who respect the elderly, and if you want to know of such an ophthalmologist, oncologist, dentist, audiologist, or general practitioner in the Monadnock Region of New Hampshire, I'd be glad to provide the names.

Nine

We are offered suggestions for successful aging, showing how we can best care for ourselves and avoid isolation and depression. The suggestions, mostly about healthy habits and doing pleasant things, seem impressive and important, but I seldom see what I believe is the most important, which is to keep tight bonds with other people or form them if you don't have them already. We are a social species. Hence, strong social bonds are crucial to the point that they're almost a species requirement, and those who lack those bonds or are unable to form them are headed for serious trouble.

Consider the evolutionary line of our ancestors from monkeys to us via the gibbon types, the ancestral chimpanzee types, the australopithecines, and *Homo erectus*. All were social species, probably intensely social species. All must have seen group membership as the key to survival. The ability to bond for mutual cooperation has kept our lineage on the planet for twenty million years.

The above might satisfy the science minded, and the religious can look to the Bible's Golden Rule, Luke 6:31: *Do to others as you would have them do to you.* At the time, the saying wasn't intended to describe an instinct, although it does. Building and maintaining relationships is probably the most important factor for our happiness and safety.

Science confirms this, but in this respect the Bible probably exceeds science, having literally hundreds of passages that promote bonding, some almost the same as Luke 6:31. Here's Matthew 7:12: *In everything do to others as you would have them do to you.* And here's Matthew 22:39: *You shall love your neighbor as yourself.* And many more.

We try to be nice people. We willingly apply the Golden Rule to our social and family connections. We willingly and naturally do unto our connections as we would have our connections do unto us, and they do, so our bonds remain tight and our warm relationships continue.

Without strong bonds, things go wrong, and I'll tell of two times when they did, one story reflecting the present, the other the distant past. The first is about a woman I'll call Mary, who spent six months as my guest. Her story shows a process of alienation and perhaps the reasons for it. It took place in recent times, and it isn't a happy story, so I've altered some details to protect this woman's privacy.

The second story shows a consequence of alienation. It's about one of the San who lived in the vast savanna wilderness we visited. It took place in the early 1950s.

MARY ASKED TO LIVE WITH ME BECAUSE SHE WAS ALONE, TEMPO-rarily unwell, and estranged from most members of her family. Although I'd known her when she was a child, I hadn't seen much of her since, but her parents had been close friends of mine and this was our connection. I said I'd love to have her.

Mary didn't pay rent or help with expenses, nor was she asked to, but that didn't seem to please her or make her feel part of the family. She never complained to me, but she hadn't been with me for long before I learned she was complaining to my assistant and housekeeper, Bella. Mary found fault with the view, with the weather, with me, with my son, with his family, with my dogs, with my cats, with the food we ate, with the way we cooked it, and even with the house itself, which she said was dirty. (This, although Bella cleaned it.) But Mary spent most of her time in the house, not going for walks, not finding a job, just watching television or sharing her complaints with Bella, who was in the house on weekdays.

Bella was kind enough to listen to Mary, so Mary began to see

Bella as someone like herself—disliking me and my family but too needy and dependent to leave. It wasn't an accurate assumption. Bella could have had any job she wanted, and we had been close friends for more than twenty years. We were puzzled by Mary's complaining and we'd wonder why she stayed.

Mary's neighbor had brought her to my house, but she'd had her car shipped to her, so she could have driven away whenever she liked. She'd sold her condo, so at least she had some money, and she was healthy, literate, and cogent, so she could have found a job. Bella and I both urged her to do this or at least to volunteer for something, anything to take her mind off her problems, but she seemed to prefer to stay in a place she disliked and spend her days disliking it.

After six months of this, I'd wonder if she planned to stay permanently. I asked her to sign a paper that said she was welcome to stay for as long as she liked, but if I died, the house would belong to my children, who might sell it, in which case she understood she'd need to find another place to live. She wanted a few changes made before she signed the paper—for instance, she wanted a two-week notice before she had to leave—so I wrote another paper with her changes.

Saying nothing, she signed it. A few days later she told us she'd bought a house in Florida, and a week after that she left.

SOME MONTHS LATER, BELLA WAS DIAGNOSED WITH A BRUTAL form of cancer and much too soon was under hospice care. One day I was visiting her, sitting on her bed, when her husband brought in the day's mail and handed her a letter. As she read it, she gasped. Then she held it by the corner as if it were toxic and handed it to me. "Read this from Mary," she said.

So I did. It went on for three pages. First, Mary praised Bella for her kindness, then she described her version of her stay. She was "enslaved," she said (she was asked to do nothing). She "never felt safe" (from my little dogs?). She was "in prison" (but could have left anytime in her car) so it was her "worst experience ever." And although she had stayed for half a year, she "couldn't get out fast enough." All that in detail and more.

I knew she'd been complaining, but this letter took the cake. I was surprised. So was Bella, and so was Wanda, who then was Bella's hospice nurse. When Wanda came to see Bella, we showed her the letter. Wanda read it. "I only wish she'd written it on Charmin so I could wipe my ass with it," she said.

We laughed long and hard. I added that Mary thought she was in prison because that's where you get six months of food and lodging free. We had a nice time laughing, but I believe that the letter, an appeal for Bella's sympathy, had alienated Mary from the three of us for life.

Mary did unto others as she wouldn't want others to do unto her, and unless she's found that this can be risky, I'm assuming she'll do it again. Most of us don't choose to be the way we are, and we don't always know how others see us. Mary probably didn't understand that continuous faultfinding was alienating, or that her letter (which she meant only for Bella) would shock Bella enough to show it to the rest of us, or that to mitigate our anger we'd have a great time making fun of her. I fear that unless she finds a better way of interpreting people, she may endure old age by herself. As for me, my effort to help her amounted to nothing, and I hope I never see her again.

IF MARY'S STORY SHOWS WHAT ALIENATION CAN LOOK LIKE, MY next story shows why we fear it, as all of us do, whether we know it or not. For our ancestors, social connections were the key to survival, and because they took care to foster these connections, the rest of us are here.

I saw this in the culture of the San, a culture designed to avoid division. Among the San, everyone was equal. No one was better or more important than anyone else, nor did anyone want to be. They had no chiefs or headmen. The children's games didn't have winners and losers. Important decisions were made by consensus, and everyone's voice was heard.

Most people had dozens of social connections, and not only through birth and marriage. People who were named for someone shared connections with that person, and many people had partnerships with others far away. The partners would exchange gifts periodically, promoting friendship and safety. If your surroundings were damaged—let's say your water hole went dry—and your partner's surroundings were strong—let's say their water hole had water—you could stay with your partner's people.

Almost everyone had dozens of connections, but we knew a man named /Gao who had just one connection, which he lost. /Gao had never married because he had never hunted success-fully, which was a prerequisite for marriage. His sister was his only living relative, thus his only connection, so he stayed with her at her husband's encampment. Since he didn't hunt, there wasn't much he could do for others, and few if any people other than his sister felt obliged to do anything for him. He knew this, of course. It made him depressed and critical, so he often did what Mary did—he criticized others, which didn't help.

One day, a group of people came to visit, and some were sick with a terrible form of flu. As it spread through the en-campment, /Gao's sister caught it. She was older than /Gao and fragile, and she died.

When someone died in an encampment, the people there would move, so her people prepared to move to another en-campment, a walk that would take them two days. My mind's eye still sees them starting off in single file, a strong man with a spear at the front of the line, another strong man with a spear at the end of it, with women, children, and other men between them, carrying babies or small children and various kinds of packs. /Gao couldn't walk as fast as the others, so he soon fell behind, naked except for his leather loincloth, his empty hands dangling at his sides.

Night came, and the people made camp. /Gao wasn't with

them. Normally when the San were on the move and someone fell behind, others would go back to find him. But nobody went back to look for /Gao. He was alone on the endless veld at night without a fire when hyenas found him.

Our need for social relationships arose from things like that.

ISOLATION IS PAINFUL FOR THOSE WHO BELONG TO SOCIAL SPEcies, and we're not the only species whose members experience the pain. When I think of isolation, I think of /Gao and Mary, but I also think of a wild turkey and a lion.

For hundreds of years, encouraged by the scientists, we have held the belief that we are the only creatures who have thoughts and emotions; but like the flat-earth theory, this theory was revised. Now it's acknowledged that when it comes to thoughts and feelings, other animals are very much like us.

Turkeys live in groups. Not only do they want one another's company, but with many pairs of eyes focused in different directions, they're safer than they are when they're alone. In this, they were like the San in the 1950s, and this was the condition of a male turkey I often saw from my office window in New Hampshire. He would walk alone around my field, a dark little figure in a vast space, eating bits of grass and looking for insects; if a group of other turkeys walked out of the woods, he'd sometimes try to join them.

He never got inside the group—he'd always be about twenty feet away—but he seemed to want to be with them or near them, because he'd follow them for a while at a distance before giving up. The others didn't seem to know he was there.

Every evening, just before dark, the flock would roost in a group of trees they favored, where they would spend the night. One evening, after the last of them was in a tree, my lone male tried to join them. But then I saw much flapping of wings, and he flew back down to the field. They seemed to have chased him away.

Turkeys have predators, of course, most of whom are nocturnal, and around the field were hundreds of trees for him to roost in, but it was almost completely dark by then and turkeys can't see well in the dark. At dawn he was still in the field, near where I'd seen him.

For two years, he tried to join others. He'd follow a group of three males that stayed together, but they too didn't want him. This year, I haven't seen him. Something must have happened to him. I felt he was something like me, and sometimes I'd put some corn out for him, but the other turkeys ate it although he was in the field before they came. Perhaps he never found it. I wish I'd done something he wanted.

I SAW THE LION IN NAMIBIA'S ETOSHA PARK WHEN I WAS THERE in the 1980s with Katharine Boynton Payne, the woman who discovered the use of infrasound by land mammals. Near a water hole, Katy had made a platform about twenty feet high from which we could record the voices of a group of elephants who came to drink at night. We were up on the platform waiting for the elephants when, in the far distance, a lion walked out of the bushes.

It was evening. The sun was low in the west. We watched the lion walk toward us. His mane was black, which meant he was old, and he walked slowly. He went to a little hill about a hundred feet from our platform, where he lay down to face the setting sun, propping himself on his elbows with his head raised and his ears stiff.

Suddenly he roared. He roared again, and again, and again, never shifting his gaze from the sun, roaring from the time it was close to the horizon until its last red flame disappeared below. Then he stood up, turned around, and slowly walked back the way he came. He must have seen us on the platform—we were very conspicuous—but he had come to roar at the sun as it was leaving, and we meant nothing. We might have been birds.

What had we seen? As has been said, lions are social. If an elderly lion is alone, it probably means the pride of lionesses that once was his has been taken in battle by another lion who was probably stronger and younger. The defeated lion may spend the rest of his life alone, with no help in hunting, doing his best to survive. There aren't many reasons for an elderly lion to be alone. It seemed to me that the lion we saw had been evicted.

We believe that roars are scary, but that's because these roars scare us. For lions, they're communications. "I'm here," they're saying. Sometimes this is meant to intimidate another lion, and sometimes it's asking for an answer. The sun didn't answer him, of course, but I think he was asking.

I live alone with a view to the west, and I also watch the sunset. It means very much to me, although I don't know why, nor can I guess what it meant to the lion, but when I watch the sun go down, I think of those in that grave on the north side of a hill—my pride, if I was a lion—and I remember the Etosha lion, wondering if he felt the way I feel while watching the sun go under.

Ten

Isolation can be a serious problem for anyone, especially for those who are aging, but books on aging don't always address it as such. This is partly because of the way we live today—in single families that come apart when children grow up and find homes of their own. This can enable isolation and is nothing like the way we lived after we evolved as the San and lived on the African savanna. There, we always had a group, the same group. It gained and lost members, of course, but the group as such was always there and solid. Today we have nothing comparably solid and must approximate the Old Way by creating temporary, personal groups of our own.

These aren't always strong or permanent, and not all of us can form them.

Certain studies, however, offer suggestions for successful aging that anyone can manage, whether isolated or not, so here I'll mention three primary ones. The first, which I'll call Suggestion One, tells us to stay healthy. Don't drink too much alcohol, don't smoke, get plenty of exercise, and eat the right foods.

Most of us know this already, and many of us obey. These are the lucky ones whose lives will be longer than the lives of those who think that because they're still breathing, they must be caring for themselves, no matter what they're doing.

Alas, I may be in the latter group. I smoke, eat whatever I find in the refrigerator except the frozen tiger turd Sy gave me (meanwhile hoping I don't get so senile that I eat the tiger turd too), and believe I'm exercising if I walk from my office to the house.

As for food, I set my own standards. For instance, I can't believe that sugar is unhealthy. I look at my hummingbirds drinking from the feeder. The liquid they suck down is 25 percent sugar, and sometimes the five tiny hummingbirds who live near my office drink half a quart a day. If they're together, they chase one another away from the little holes they drink from—the feeder has eight little holes and only five birds drink from them, so it's unclear what they fight about—but if one bird is alone with no competition for a little hole, he may drink for an entire minute. You can drink an enormous amount in one minute—try it yourself—and I know he's drinking because his throat moves when he swallows.

These tiny birds are filled with sugar, and it seems to work for them. In the fall they fly from New Hampshire to Panama, and in the spring they fly back. Anyone who can do that is healthy—of this there is no doubt. My brain is saying, *You're not a hummingbird.* My answer is, *So what?*

As for exercise, I was forced to improve. I've been invited to go to Thailand to see dholes. What are dholes? They're *Cuon alpinus,* the Asiatic version of wolves. I'd be going with a small group of people including my dear friend Sy, and one needs to be able to walk five miles to qualify.

When I heard this requirement, I huffed. Five miles? I walked seventy-five miles across Baffin Island. *But Liz,* said my brain, *then you were forty. Now you're over eighty.* This was true. *But I really want to go,* I said. *Then you must prepare,* my brain replied, and I realized that walking from my office to the house wouldn't do it. So I began to walk half a mile a day, from my house to the end of the road and back, and as I walk I not only prepare for Thailand, I also satisfy the exercise requirement.

As for smoking, it's said that two-thirds of smokers die from smoking, which means that one-third of us don't. At the time of this writing I'm reasonably healthy, having lived almost 31,968 days, with a heart that's beat more than 3,658,176,000 times, and in the last forty years I've smoked 292,000 cigarettes, so I tell myself I'm in that lucky third.

Actually, in addition to glaucoma I'm getting macular de-generation, which also ruins your eyesight and is made worse by smoking, but I'm not talking about my eyesight now, and yes, I know I'm awful. If I'm about to die or if I'm dead when this book is published, I'm hoping the publisher will put THE AUTHOR DIED OF BAD HABITS in big red letters under my name on the cover.

Even so, my favorite photo is of an elderly woman at her hundredth birthday party, lighting a cigarette from a candle on the cake. For my eightieth birthday I wanted a photo of me doing this, but my children wouldn't have it. "Put that camera away," they told me.

Did I just call them "children"? They're bossy grown-ups. I put the camera away.

FOR A PLEASANT OLD AGE, SUGGESTION ONE IS GOOD, BUT NOT always easy to manage. Suggestion Two is better. "Do some-thing," it says. And here retirement can be a problem, or it can for some.

If for all your adult life you've had a job and suddenly must leave it, you could find yourself alone in the daytime, trying to understand what the ads on television are promoting. Or you might become like Mary, looking out the window at your neighbors, noticing that weeds grow on their lawn. Hope-fully, you'll have a dog you can take for a walk or a cat who will sit on your lap and purr for you, but it won't be like your earlier days when you worked alongside others toward a common goal.

Some were your friends. When you'd arrive at work in the morning, you'd be glad to see them. You'd have lunch together. Now the only person you see is yourself in the mirror. You're supposed to feel positive, but how can you? Your life is a lonely bad dream.

FOR OTHERS, RETIREMENT IS AN OPPORTUNITY. YOU CAN TRAVEL. You might go to Paris and see the Eiffel Tower. You might take a tourist safari in Namibia and see a lion. Or a lioness. Or a lion and four lionesses eating a kudu. You might watch a baboon approach you, wondering if he can snatch the cracker you're eating. Or you might play golf every day and improve your game.

You might volunteer at a shelter for the homeless or at a church or a hospital to help those less fortunate than yourself. You might run for public office. You might win the election. Or you might lie on a beach and listen to the sweep of breaking waves.

The beach you're on could be in Costa Rica. When you tire of the beach, you could visit a forest where you might see a spider monkey or a quetzal with red and green feathers and a long green tail. You'd think of the job you left, the noisy workplace you retired from. You might have purchased hearing aids and would enjoy the quetzal's musical high-pitched song.

Or you might stay home and start a vegetable garden. Every day you'd be sure your plants had enough water, no parasites to bother them, and no weeds for competition. Your guests would praise your summer squash when they ate it at your birthday party.

One important study clearly shows that after retirement the people who did something they enjoyed led pleasant lives. If your funding is secure and your health isn't failing, and if you choose what you want to do and then keep doing it, your retirement could be the best part of your life.

AND NOW FOR SUGGESTION THREE. THIS SAYS, "DON'T BE ISO-lated," and as I've tried to show with my stories of Mary and /Gao, also of the turkey and the lion, this may be the most important. We're a great ape, and all of us except orangutans are programmed to be social.

But old widows like me often find themselves alone. I cope by leaving the television on, so I hear human voices, and by having two dogs and three cats. All are males, I'm the only female, but that doesn't seem to matter. We all sleep in the same bed and all of us are happy, our warm bodies pressed close.

Even so, in the morning I often feel depressed, although this fades when I'm working in my office. There, I live in the time and place I'm writing about, which normally is nice, but not always. The subject of this book, for instance, could add to the depression, because it stops me from ignoring my symptoms of old age. If my next book isn't about commas, it may be about sunshine and flowers.

Meanwhile, I'm grateful that my son and his family live across the road, that I have friends, and that I have a landline telephone, so I can talk with my daughter in Texas whenever I want without looking for an area with cell-phone signals. All of this is enjoyable, and I do better if I retain this mindset and ban the thoughts and memories that make me lonely or sad.

I'm glad to serve on two town committees, because at the meetings I'm with interesting people whom I admire but don't know very well. When I'm with them, I'm in a normal, social environment, talking about nonpersonal issues that require thought and study. It's a bit like getting hearing aids. It puts me in the real world.

But life alone can be disastrous for some of us. Wanda provides home care for such people and tells me that some live in miserable quarters—dirty and messy, with a lack of good food because food requires shopping, with clothes unwashed and showers not taken because it's hard to get dressed and undressed and easier to sleep in your clothes. Wanda once told me that so many fleas lived in one of these houses that, before she went inside, she put dog flea collars around her ankles. She also called Protective Services, which helps those who have difficulty managing their lives.

If left alone, conditions like those mentioned here get

worse as time passes. The disorganized house becomes your ecosystem. Nobody wants to visit you. You'll be alone for most of the time, and this will keep you depressed.

EVEN SO, MANY OF US WANT TO STAY IN OUR HOUSES. WHEN WE begin our physical and mental deterioration, we can often find people such as Wanda to help us. Or perhaps a family member will live with us, or we will live with a family member.

My dad did that. I think of him in his last years. By then his mind was mostly gone, but, dressed in pajamas and a bathrobe, delusional but comfortable, he would sit by my mother in her office while she wrote two books. I often visited my parents, and although my dad didn't always know me, he always knew my mother, and he always seemed happy and content when he was with her. If he'd been in a nursing home, he might have wandered, perhaps in an effort to find her, so he would have been locked up.

At home he could have wandered, but he didn't. He was glad to sit beside her. He and my mother took care of their mothers, my mother took care of him, I took care of my husband's mother, also my mother, also my husband, and if all goes well, my children will take care of me. In the old days, we didn't have choices, and our family keeps these customs. *Stay together*, our instincts remind us. *Stay together. Take care of your own.*

Not everyone can do this. The people I've mentioned above,

starting with my grandmothers and ending with me, had children who loved them. But what if you don't have children? What if you do, but they turned out to be selfish little rats who don't care about you? What if they live in other countries or are somehow compromised in such a way that they can't help you? What if no matter where they are or what they're like, you don't want to burden them? What do you do then?

If you decide to stay in your home, you'll be fine as long as you're healthy and reasonably cogent. If your health starts to fail, you will probably be able to find an agency that provides visiting nurses. We had this for my husband. A nurse came in the morning to help him get up and again in the evening to help him go to bed. During the day he had the rest of us to help him, which won't be true for me if I decide to stay at home.

In that case, I'll still have responsibility for the house and all this involves, and that's a bit of a burden, especially if I'm not reasonably cogent. I see myself forgetting to get my car inspected or fumbling through drawers in search of a credit card I'd unknowingly left at the market. For serious confusion, we clearly need help, and this from someone we can trust absolutely, as no one is easier to rob or cheat than an elderly person whose mind is failing.

THIS BRINGS US TO RETIREMENT COMMUNITIES, ALSO KNOWN AS senior living communities. Again, I'm planning to live at home or with my children, but my daughter has no children, nor do some of my dearest friends, and I imagine them in one of these communities, confident that they'll be happy there.

Nothing is perfect, including these communities, so I'll present some of the problems, but I also hope to show their value, because for some of us, these communities are an important answer, often the best answer, sometimes the only answer, to our aging well.

Eleven

What are senior living communities like? In most of them, the residential areas consist of cottages or apartments of various sizes with one or two bedrooms, a bathroom, a living room, and a little kitchen. These are for people who can care for themselves. For those who can't, most communities have assisted-living areas. Most people in these areas have some form of dementia, and the entrances are locked so the people won't wander away.

Some communities also have quarters staffed with nurses for those who need medical care. Many communities with all these features will keep you from the day you enter until the day you die, but a community without these features will make you leave or will transport you elsewhere if, for some reason, you're failing.

I knew a husband and wife who had lived together in one of the latter communities until the husband became ill and was transferred to a nursing home in another town. He died alone, and a day or two went by before his wife learned she was a widow.

The communities that keep you permanently—more formally known as "continuing care retirement communities"—tend to be somewhat more expensive than those that ship you out. But if you can afford to live in a keeper community, it seems worth it, because by the time you need more help, you may not be able to relocate yourself, which means that a community employee might do it for you, and you may not have a choice about where you end up. This happened to several people I knew or knew about. For one couple the husband ended up in New Hampshire and the wife in Massachusetts. Neither was able to drive, so they seldom saw each other.

WHILE DOING RESEARCH FOR THIS BOOK, I VISITED THE VARIOUS kinds of communities in our area. I was shown around the residential areas, but I didn't see as much of the assisted-living areas or the nursing areas, as these of course are private, as they should be. However, my two friends who worked in nursing homes described these places for me, and once I went to one of them to visit a friend who was a patient.

The friends who were nurses assumed it was normal for

things to go well, so they didn't have much to say about that, but they did tell me about the mistakes and problems, which of course concerned them. I was told that in one nursing home, a woman with dementia attacked a man in a wheelchair, clubbing him hard on the head with her cane. She'd clubbed him five or six times before a caregiver ran up to pull her away. After that she was kept in a locked area.

In the nursing home I visited, I saw for myself what might be a problem, at least for some. Each room had two beds; thus almost everyone had a roommate. Each room also had a television set, and I wondered what it would be like if your roommate watched television constantly. What if the roommate was a sports fan and you didn't like sports? Or what if he or she was hard of hearing, didn't have hearing aids, and kept the sound way up?

Interestingly, the friend I was visiting soon described what that was like, because she'd had the experience. The problem was solved when she was moved to another room. It wasn't a single room—two beds were in it—but nobody was in the other bed. This woman recovered and now is in her own home. Her experience in the nursing home was good, she says.

MOST OF THE PROBLEMS, OR SO I WAS TOLD, ARISE FROM UNDER-staffing. I found one assisted-living area with thirty patients but only two caregivers, each with fifteen patients in her care. Perhaps this is the norm. One morning a man began asking for help to get in his wheelchair so he could get to the bathroom.

But the caregiver was helping a patient take a shower and another patient was ringing for help to get dressed, so after a very long wait, the man tried to get in his wheelchair by himself. He fell, pulling the wheelchair on top of himself. He was injured and wet his pants.

Falls, I was told, are the most serious problem. But medication errors also occur. A medication may be given at the wrong time, or the wrong medication may be given accidentally. Or the right medication may be in the attendant's hand as she stands by the bed of the person who needs it, but she can't give it because it's new for the patient and can't be offered until the doctor who prescribed it informs the manager of the nursing home of what he has prescribed.

A final problem, at least in this list, is that people whose mental faculties are failing are prime targets for thieves. A woman who might not remember that she ever owned a pearl necklace and wouldn't know if it was missing would be easy to rob. Or if she claimed that it was stolen, others might think she'd forgotten that she'd given it away.

A version of this happened to my mother when she was living alone in Cambridge before she lived with me. A caregiver from a nursing facility came to help her every day, and I later learned that the caregiver had badgered my mother into visiting her safe-deposit box at the bank. My mother was experiencing considerable confusion, so the people at the bank were uncomfortable, but the caregiver prodded my mother to reassure them, and eventually they let them both in. The caregiver accompanied my mother to a closed room where they opened her safe-deposit box and left with her most valuable possessions, including a gold necklace and a magnetron ring. She also took my mother's silver platter, too big to fit in the box.

The ring was made by my father. Magnetrons are used for radar, and my father's company made the magnetrons used in radar during World War II. Thus, there was no other ring like it, and many years later a friend of ours saw it on the caregiver's finger. The caregiver lived next door to our friend's sister, and he'd gone to his sister's for a visit. When he happened to see the caregiver, he recognized the ring. She must have sold the necklace and the silver platter, and she told him my mother had given her the ring. But we could do nothing about it—my mother was no longer living, and years had passed before we learned of the theft.

I'VE PRESENTED A SHORT COLLECTION OF SOME OF THE PROBLEMS, but I can't think of anywhere that wouldn't have some sort of problems, including my own home, so I continued my visits to the retirement communities. I managed to visit five of them, I learned a great deal about all of them, and I know what to look for if I need to live in one.

First, I should discuss the costs. These seemed high, so to gauge this I looked at the cost of living at home. I pay a heavy property tax because I live in New Hampshire, which seems to get all its money for everything from property taxes. I pay a king's ransom for winter fuel. I have a two-story house that in 1935 was built for six grown-ups and two children; later an apartment with its own furnace was added for my mother, and in both parts the pipes could freeze if unheated, so that's two furnaces that run all winter and require plenty of fuel. I also pay large bills for electricity, phone, and internet service. My water comes from my own well, so I don't pay for water, but I pay to have the septic tank pumped and the water filter changed.

I pay a friend to mow the fields, and when my son is away I pay someone to mow the lawn, since the lawn is big and the mower is heavy and now I can't mow the lawn myself.

In winter, I pay to have our driveway sanded, although my son plows the snow, and I recently paid to fix the garage roof. I will soon need to fix the roof of the house, although that will be so expensive I keep putting it off. The roof leaks only when it rains, but even so I must find the funds to fix it soon.

To make a long story short, it adds up, so when I compare the cost of maintaining my house to the cost of a retirement community, the retirement community seems reasonable.

IN SOME RESIDENTIAL COMMUNITIES, YOU PAY AN APPLICATION fee—in one case it's $2,250. Years may pass before they admit you, and when they do, you pay a one-time entrance fee. In one facility the entrance fee is between $38,400 and $47,800, depending on the quarters you've chosen. In another it's between $309,000 and $365,000. To me this sounds like "Sell your house and give us the money," but most of these communities are full.

However, the highest entrance fees are charged by communities that keep the residents for life, even if a resident runs out of money, and heavy entrance fees take care of some of that. Part of the entrance fee may be returned if the resident moves away or dies soon after arriving.

Once you're there you also pay a monthly fee—in one facility it's between $3,169 and $5,835, depending on your quarters, and in another it's between $6,485 and $9,612. These costs are for one person. Since the costs are mostly for services, they almost double for two people. (Again, please remember how much it costs to live at home. Not that much, but plenty just the same.) Some communities offer three meals a day, but at least one of them offers just one meal a day, your choice.

Your cottage or apartment will have a little kitchen where you can cook for yourself, but you must buy your own food at a market. And in New Hampshire, if your community has nursing quarters, you also pay your share of a "granny tax" (note the derogatory name) charged by the state for its quality assessment of the nursing section. You also pay more to stay in a nursing section, where you are charged for such items as catheters, bandages, and other medically related items you may need.

To make sure you'll be able to pay the expenses, these facilities thoroughly examine your finances when you apply, and you must provide total information. So not only are these places expensive, they're also nosy. But a community that keeps you if you run out of money needs to know when this might happen. If you could run out of money in a few years, they probably wouldn't take you.

Many people can't afford residential communities. Some low-income elderly apply for affordable housing offered in certain apartment buildings. The federal government pays a portion of the rent, but the quarters are just apartments and are open to people of all ages, the requirement being an income below 30 percent of the area's median income—a requirement that many older people meet. The apartments I know about are well kept and in good condition, but pets are seldom if ever allowed and the landlords don't offer any kind of care.

If care is needed, Medicare or Medicaid may pay for nursing care offered by several of the companies that send nurses to your house or apartment. Medicare pays for one hundred days of skilled care but after that, you're on your own. And then, if your condition is severe or permanent, you may be sent to a nursing home where, if you're out of money, you stay for free, but the nursing home takes your Social Security payments. Even so, many elderly people apply for these apartments. The waiting time can be up to nine years.

If I can afford it, I'd rather be in a retirement community than in affordable housing, although I wasn't sure I'd want to be in a retirement community when I started looking into them. On my first visits, I was just doing the usual research, so I felt only mild professional interest. Someone from the management would show me around, we'd look at this and that, and I'd write a few notes when we finished.

I did like the care they took to keep the residents from boredom. All the communities offered lectures, films, or various other diversions; they also had exercise rooms, libraries, and bars. In the dining rooms they'd seat you wherever you wanted, whether with friends or by yourself, and the food was said to be excellent—two of these communities had French chefs to do the cooking and bad food was not reported in the others. All this was interesting, all this was nice, but I was just looking, not planning to sign up.

Then in one community, my guide showed me a room used for hobbies. She told me that some of the women did embroidery together and showed me their table covered with colorful threads. *Ho hum*, I thought. *Who wants to embroider? I'd rather rub dirt on my head.*

Then suddenly I understood what I was seeing. I pictured myself sitting alone in my upstairs bedroom, looking at the floor, and realized there was nothing I'd rather do than some embroidery. I'd be with other people, they'd teach me how to do it, we'd talk and laugh, and I'd have a good time and be happy. And while I was sewing, I wouldn't be worrying about household problems such as my generator making carbon monoxide, or the mice in my basement biting the electric wires and starting fires, or how much snow I'd need to shovel after the next winter storm.

When I learned that dogs and cats are welcome in that community, I was almost ready to sign up. The only problem was that smoking isn't allowed in this or any other community. In one, you couldn't even smoke on the property, which meant you'd be walking about a quarter of a mile at night in bitter winter weather just to smoke a cigarette. That would have been enough to discourage me, except that if I live with my nonsmoking son or my nonsmoking daughter, I won't be able to smoke in their homes either. But I wouldn't have to go far to smoke—I'd just step out the door and light up.

So I haven't decided. I might live with my son or my daughter—a solution to aging that we've used for hundreds of years—or I might sign up for a residential community. But the main reason I'm interested in the various communities is because I want the childless people who are dear to me to know that such places are available. My friends in these communities thoroughly enjoy their lives, and I know it's good to live there, cared for, making new friends, and free of most responsibilities.

So if you think of looking into this, here's some advice. Decide the area you want to live in and visit the retirement communities. Ask if there's a health requirement. Ask if there's a financial requirement. (There almost always is.) Whoever shows you around will tell you that everyone is happy and that old age can be joyous, but this, although it's often true, has a hint of sales talk about it, so ask for a booklet that describes the community (every community has a booklet). The booklet won't reveal the problems, but some, such as expenses your guide didn't mention, may be suggested by what you learn. Then look at some of the apartments.

I did this at all the communities I visited and found that the smallest, least expensive apartments were more than big enough for me—one person with two little dogs and two or three cats.

If I go there, I'll try to get an apartment on the ground floor, so I can put the dogs on leashes and walk out the door (no stairs, no elevator). My cats became indoor cats when they began to hunt birds, but I'll put a table under a window where they can sit and bird-watch.

Ask if money is refunded if you die before you've spent the time you paid for, and if so, under what circumstances. Find out the ratio of patients to caregivers in the assisted-living and nursing sections, although the ratio may change over time. See if the lectures, films, and other events that are offered will entertain you. And find out if you can keep your dogs or cats or both. Several communities don't allow pets, and some allow you to bring your pet when you move there but forbid you to get another if yours dies.

Service dogs by law cannot be rejected. However, while service dogs themselves must be accepted, these communities are not required to accept their owners, which perhaps is why when visiting most of these communities, the only species seen is *Homo sapiens*. This can be tragic, because many of us are deeply attached to our pets, and to prevent us from having them is cruelty. Most of us think that this is okay, but some of us think we should change our name to *Homo not very sapiens*, because *sapiens* means *wise*.

SOME OF THE ABOVE MAY APPEAR AS NEGATIVE, SO NOW I WILL offer the most important evidence about these residential communities, which comes from friends now living in them. One of these friends had been on a cruise, which she thought was perfect—lots of excitement, great food, and no problems. She said that to be in the retirement community was like being on a cruise. All kinds of events were offered, she told me, something different every day, and she greatly enjoyed being there.

Another friend said that living in one of these communities is like being in college. I've never been on a cruise, so to me this recommendation was the most compelling. The experience is relatively new to everyone, everyone is in the same age group under the same conditions, everyone makes new friends, who, with lifetimes of interesting experiences, are fairly sure to be interesting people. In fact, it's even better than college. The people are there to enjoy themselves, so they're not required to learn anything or forced to take exams.

SO IF THESE COMMUNITIES INTEREST YOU, DO THE RESEARCH BEfore the time comes when you may need to go there. Don't worry about the problems I've mentioned above. Most of these things (like falling or wetting your pants) will happen anyway, no matter where you are. Don't wait to be in your late eighties, wishing you were in a residential community. Look into them while you're younger. You won't need to live there right away, but you should learn about them to prepare. Find out the probable waiting period. In some places, you can sign up in advance and will be notified when an apartment of your choice becomes available. You can take it then or wait longer, and you'll still be at the top of the list. But find out about this first.

And don't worry too much about what to do with your house. Some of these communities have experts who can help you decide what to bring with you and what to sell or give away and can also advise you about selling your house if that's your plan. Trust me. I'm facing that problem. It's vastly easier to do this with help than to do it by yourself.

I was reminded of retirement communities when, at two o'clock one morning, I was awakened by a serious chest pain on my left side. I took my pulse and felt nothing. Then I felt blood pulsing fast but faintly, and after that I again felt nothing while the chest pain got worse.

This can't be good, I told myself and wondered what to do about it. I might have called my son—he lives across the road—but he and his family were away, so I was alone with others to care for—my two dogs and my son's dog, also my three cats and my son's cat, who is diabetic. The cats had litter boxes, but the dogs didn't, and in a few hours they would need to go outside to pee and then would need their breakfast, as would the cats, and the diabetic cat would need his insulin injection. I didn't know who would care for them if I drove myself to the local ER (this seemed unwise) or called 911 and was whisked off by an ambulance. Anyway, the doors of my house were locked, so the ambulance people couldn't get in.

I thought of calling my friend Nancy Folsom. She's a nurse, but because she works hard and needs her rest and also was at least twenty minutes away, I didn't want to wake her in the middle of the night. I don't know my neighbors very well, nice as they are, and anyway they live at a distance and I don't know their phone numbers. My son's family was away, and my daughter lives in Texas. They wouldn't be able to help me, so I didn't think I should call them just to frighten them. What should I do?

WHAT I DID WAS WISH I WAS IN A RETIREMENT COMMUNITY. I'D know who to call, and help would come quickly. One has no such option when alone and far from other people. What if my heart had stopped, not just briefly but forever? In a retirement community, this would soon be noticed. At home, days could go by before anyone might notice. The dogs would have relieved themselves indoors, the cat who needs insulin would have missed his injections, and he, the other cats, and the dogs would be thirsty and starved.

Obviously, the problem passed, and here I am, writing about it. I don't know exactly what happened to me, but whatever it was, it's gone, and I'll go to see my doctor. But if I lived in a retirement community and had a heart attack, professional help would be obvious and ready. What happened to me could happen to anyone anywhere, not always with a happy ending. It's worth considering.

Twelve

The conclusion of old age is death, and because we have conflicting views about it, it merits some discussion. The poet Dylan Thomas (no relation) famously wrote:

Do not go gentle into that good night,
Old age should burn and rave at close of day;
Rage, rage against the dying of the light.

Loud raging can discourage a listener, so the poem's last line suggests that someone or something will hear you raging and perhaps get scared and back off. Although the amount of rage the poem is promoting would not discourage a large predatory mammal such as *Dinofelis*—the prehistoric "terrible cat" who preyed on our ancestors—it might discourage a midsized predatory mammal such as a hyena or a Grim Reaper.

The command is also advice, and although it didn't seem to work for Dylan Thomas—he was young when he wrote the poem, and he died just before he turned forty—in a quiet, modest way I take it. I don't exactly rage even though my metaphoric light is dying, but without really knowing why, I get a flu shot every autumn and take vitamin C. I try not to eat too much salt or sugar. (Well, I try not to eat too much salt. I'm sometimes a little careless about the sugar.) I have an annual physical exam, I drive with my eyes on the road and my mind on the traffic, I never text while driving, and I seldom speed. Somewhere inside me, without really knowing what I'm doing, I'm trying to avoid the Grim Reaper.

BUT THAT'S MY UNCONSCIOUS AT WORK—MY INSTINCTS FROM THE deep, deep past. Consciously, I'm not afraid of dying, although I'm cautious. When I'm working at night and getting tired, I finish the page or the paragraph or the chapter I'm writing, because what if I died in my sleep and left it half finished? My brilliant ideas would be lost!

But death as such doesn't frighten me, if only because I've cheated death four times. One was a plane crash in the then Belgian Congo that would have killed me along with all the other passengers if I'd been on board and hadn't changed my reservation, and another was when, while in the Kalahari, my mother and I were struck by lightning, which threw us to the ground. At the time, we didn't know that the place where we were staying was called "Place of Lightning" (*Tcho!'ana* in the Ju/'hoan language) and didn't even know we'd been struck by lightning until someone who'd seen it happen told us. We just wondered why we were suddenly lying side by side, flat on our faces on the ground.

My third escape was thanks to my speed when a lioness charged at me. Again I was in Etosha Park participating in the study of elephant infrasound. I took the van to pick up some equipment we'd left behind and found a lioness lying beside it. Knowing what the San would do (although probably not in that circumstance), I got out of the van and approached her respectfully, calling her Old Lioness and asking her to move. She charged.

You're not supposed to run from lions—it only excites them—but this time I didn't think I had a choice. I ran faster than I ever ran before and jumped in the van. She wasn't ten feet away when the van door slammed behind me. She then slowed down, seemed indifferent, and walked away at an oblique angle without looking back. She knew I'd leave if she scared me but she probably would have killed me if I stood still. Lions think nothing of killing. They kill something every few days, and it's hard to imagine she wouldn't have killed me.

One thing I gathered from the experience is that being

killed by a lion would be interesting. I'd learn an enormous amount in just a few seconds. Would she bite me in the neck as she might if I were an antelope? Would she use her claws? Would she seem angry or happy or overly hungry? Or would she just be preparing an ordinary meal? But of course I'd be dead and couldn't write about what I discovered.

My latest escape took place after a snowstorm when my son was plowing my driveway with his pickup. He would push forward, then lift the plow and back up, then lower the plow and go forward again. As he began to reverse, looking back through the left-side mirror, I stepped out of my office and found myself behind the truck's right rear corner where the mirror didn't show me. Bang! The truck knocked me down.

What happened next seemed to take forever. The truck was coming backward at three or four miles an hour, the truck's corner that hit me was only about two feet from the rear wheel, and I was lying on my left side, horrified by how badly my son would feel if he ran over his mother. Should I roll to the right and be beside the wheel so the truck would go past me, or roll to the left and be between the wheels so the truck would go over me? I actually remember these thoughts and options, but the process must have taken just a millionth of a second, because I rolled to the right and was instantly passed by the right rear tire as it brushed the sleeve of my coat. I was still rolling, which was good because the truck was turning slightly to the left and the right front tire just missed me.

I was amazed by the experience, mostly because I had so

many thoughts in much less than one second. If I'd spoken the thoughts instead of thinking them, both right tires would have squashed me. I was up on my feet before my son drove forward. He was unaware of the event, and I didn't want to tell him.

SO NOW, AFTER ALL THOSE ESCAPES, I'M MOSTLY IN TOTAL DENIAL, and this allows me to smoke.

That said, I should talk about smoking again. When I spoke of it earlier, I didn't say enough. If you're a smoker and want to live to old age, the most important thing you can do is stop. Dozens of studies prove this without question.

Even so, I can't seem to quit, although I've tried a few times. And here's where denial is damaging. I tell myself if smoking kills me, it won't be today, and if I get cancer, I'll be in the hands of a highly praised oncologist named Dr. Steven Larmon, who actually cares about his patients and looked after me when I had breast cancer.

Everyone loves him, including me, so I won't mind having more cancer, or so I tell myself, especially since the breast cancer episode went well. I just went to a hospital in Boston, where they whacked off the breast and got all the cancer. I could have gone home the next day except that I got a wound infection from the surgery (maybe the doctor hadn't washed his hands), so I had to stay a day longer.

I didn't need chemo or radiation, and being cancer-free was nice, but I didn't learn from the experience, and sometimes at night I hear the Grim Reaper rustling around outside my window. *Gosh, Liz,* my brain whispers, *don't you realize you had cancer? Dr. Larmon always asks if you've stopped smoking, and you haven't!*

WHILE WRITING THIS BOOK AND FEELING OBLIGED TO INCLUDE smoking as an undesirable practice, I talked myself into stopping again. I haven't done it yet, but I'm thinking about it. However, this isn't because I fear death, or so I tell myself; it's because I'm getting macular degeneration.

Smoking makes macular degeneration worse. When you're dead, you're at peace, or so they tell us, so it doesn't sound so bad, but macular degeneration makes you blind. To become blind when you're already feeble and confused is a totally different experience, not one that could be called "peace."

The trick will be to buy no cigarettes and make sure I have no cigarette butts in my wastebaskets or my pockets. Even so, I know I'll make a mental map of our town's streets and sidewalks. Often, cigarette butts can be found there, with tobacco in most of them. I'm not sure I'd risk the indignity of picking them up because someone might see me, but the scattered butts, those potential smoking experiences, will stay in my mind, and no matter how bad my memory becomes, I'll remember where they are if little else.

You'd be surprised by the amount of tobacco that can be left in a cigarette butt—sometimes almost a quarter of an inch, which amounts to two or three drags. Since I can't be sure I won't pick them up, I've planned what to do if someone sees me. I'll look at the person with surprise, as if I can't imagine why anyone would find fault, and I'll say I'm cleaning the street.

HERE AGAIN, I MUST EMPHASIZE THAT, AS I SEE IT, THIS ISN'T about living longer. I've already ruined my body by smoking. I will probably die of it anyway. I'll stop smoking to save my eyesight, not because I'm worried about dying.

But if that's true, why does my interest sometimes perk at the mention of a life-prolonging product? For instance, not long ago while waiting to see my doctor for my annual physical exam, I saw a magazine on the waiting-room table and opened it to an ad for such a product. The ad showed a hefty man in late middle age facing a beautiful woman with white hair and smooth skin. They're holding hands and she's showing her teeth, grinning at the man because the product will help them live longer.

Considering their somewhat youthful appearance—anything less than eighty seems youthful to me—the word "longer" might mean one thing to them and another thing to me, so I kept reading, hoping to learn more, my interest growing, until I came to the bottom of the page—the warnings. These were written in print so small that old people could hardly see them, let alone read them—a clever move on the part of the company that makes the product. Although they're required to add the warnings, if elderly people could read them, the company's best customers might be scared away.

I held the magazine close to my nose and made out that the product can damage your lungs, your intestines, and your liver, also your pituitary gland, your adrenal glands, and your pancreas. It can cause inflammation of your skin, your kidneys, and even your brain. It can make you deaf, or blind, or deaf *and* blind. I thought there might be treatment for some of the reactions until I saw the last one listed, which was "death."

Gosh. To swallow one of these pills would be like pointing a six-shooter loaded with an unknown number of bullets at your head and pulling the trigger. I'd be in bad shape if I got even one of the reactions, so rather than begging the doctor to prescribe this product for me, I forgot its name and put the magazine back on the table. I think this shows I deal with the idea of death by denying it, not by raging at it. If my instincts prevailed, I'd try the product regardless of risk, like snatching at a straw when you're drowning.

I once tried Chantix to stop smoking—a costly product that might extend your life a little. It causes nothing worse than sleepwalking, serious skin reactions, dizziness, nausea, vomiting, anxiety, frustration, irritability, anger, also depression with suicidal thoughts and suicide attempts. A suicide attempt isn't as bad as a suicide success, but even so, I was discouraged. What do I do when feeling discouraged? I light a cigarette.

Thirteen

The deaths I fear are those of others. At my stage of life, you read the obituaries in the local paper, hoping you don't see one of your friends. Too often you do, but your life goes on as always, or seems to, no matter how stricken you are when these deaths occur. The ability to trudge onward, no matter what, is a skill the elderly develop. Without it, I doubt that we'd manage. So it's not that deaths of loved ones don't affect us deeply, but by the time we're old, we're imprinted with what we're supposed to do and just keep doing it. What else should we do? Lie on the floor, screaming and kicking?

No. We note the date of the funeral because we plan to attend it. Then we empty the dishwasher and put the dishes away.

Losing a loved one can begin as early as childhood. When I was starting grade school, my mother's mother, Gran, died of Christian Science. She was only in her sixties, but she had cancer, and although she didn't proselytize Christian Science the way my other grandmother, Nana, proselytized evangelical fundamentalism, she kept the Christian Science doctrine and believed her faith would protect her.

Although Gran lived with us in Massachusetts, she was in California visiting her sister (whom we called Aunt Maggie) when her symptoms became obvious. Aunt Maggie took Gran to a hospital, where they learned that the cancer had spread throughout her body and was advanced and inoperable. Aunt Maggie phoned my mother.

That's another event I'll always remember. I was in the next room when my mother answered the phone, and soon I heard her rustling things quickly in her closet and then heard her running down the stairs. I looked over the bannister and saw her with a suitcase, running out the door. I looked out the window and saw her getting in a taxi. Months would pass before I saw her again.

Also living with us in Cambridge were the Finnish couple mentioned earlier, Tom and Kirsti Johnson, who were surrogate parents to my brother and me, doing the housekeeping and looking after me and my brother when our parents were away. We missed our mom and our Gran when they were in

California and had little concept of why they were there, so we decided to send them a letter. We could write a few words such as "bug" and "cat," but we couldn't write a letter, so Tom would take dictation. But what to write about?

By then we knew what "death" meant, but Gran was alive. And "alive" meant living as we knew it, a life without sorrow or problems. Tom had recently taken us to the zoo, where we'd seen an elephant. While we were staring at this awesome creature, she curved her tail upward, bent her hind legs slightly, and pushed out three large turds. We'd never seen anything like it. We laughed and cheered. Confident that Gran and our mother would want to know about this, we shared the experience in our letter.

At the time, we called urine "baba"—our youthful attempt at "bathroom"—and bowel movements "movies," which is why we'd be puzzled when friends would tell our parents they'd seen an excellent movie. They might name the producer or the theater where they'd seen it, and often enough our parents would say they'd like to see it too.

We saw an elephant's movies. We laughed as she produced them, laughed more as we dictated our letter, and ended the letter by describing the funniest part of the experience with a sentence I remember to this day: "The movies resounded plop, plop, plop." How's that for humor? Even Tom was laughing.

Gran and our mom knew what "movie" meant to us, and because back then it took a while for a letter to get from Massachusetts to California, a week or so later our mom called

Tom to tell him they disapproved of the vulgarity. Somehow, I learned of this but couldn't quite identify what we'd done that was wrong. I still didn't realize that Gran was dying, even though I'd seen my mother run out of the house.

Gran's family had lived in California, and she was buried with her husband, who had died there when my mother was a child. I missed Gran painfully, but my life went on normally—going to school, trying to read the funnies, making little model dinosaurs, and playing with my brother, pretending that we were raccoons. Even so, children can internalize things without knowing it, and thirty years later, one night when I was falling asleep, I heard Gran say "Elizabeth" as clearly as if she was in the room. And wasn't she? Her voice was inside me, the same after all those years.

IF ANYONE WENT TO HEAVEN, IT WAS MY FATHER'S MOTHER, Nana. She died when I was in my early twenties and she was 105. I'd gone with my mother to our house in New Hampshire, and Nana was at home in Cambridge with her caregiver, who phoned to tell us she was failing. We rushed to the car and sped toward Cambridge, but on the way we stopped at a pay phone to call the caregiver. She told us that Nana was gone.

We accepted this in silence. We'd known it would happen, and it did. In silence we drove on more slowly. But no sooner did I hear the news than I wondered how we'd get along without our Nana, and I miss her to this day. She was a gifted seamstress, and she taught me how to sew. I still have her sewing machine, an ancient model with a foot pedal. I threaded needles for her, not only for the sewing machine but also for the artfully embroidered items such as bedspreads that she sewed for us by hand.

Now I'm the age she was when she needed my help, and thanks to her I'm also pretty good at sewing. Every time I aim the tip of a thread at the eye of a needle, Nana is sitting beside me. She spent her life with us trying to persuade us to accept Christ as our Savior, and we couldn't, so I hope she accepted our failure as something God wanted, and that God's will was done.

MY FATHER DIED IN NOVEMBER 1980 WHEN HE WAS NINETY-ONE and I was forty-nine. He'd suffered from an undiagnosed brain disorder that might have been Alzheimer's. Or perhaps he was diagnosed but forgot the diagnosis.

One day when I was alone with him, vacuuming the hallway, he thought I was a terrorist with a bomb. On another day I found him walking naked on the rim of the bathtub, the same tub I'd been in when I learned what happened to our Cousin Emily, my first experience with death.

I was supposedly taking care of him that day, but while I was doing something else, unknown to me he had taken a shower. He and the bathtub were dripping wet, and he was walking sideways along the bathtub's wet curved rim, which stood at least two feet above the wet tiled floor. He was smiling, and his arms were out slightly to balance himself, but there was nothing he could grab if he wobbled. I was terrified he'd fall, but I didn't dare reach out because his reaching for me could unbalance him, so all I could do was position myself to break his fall if he fell forward. He balanced along the entire length of the bathtub's wet rim and stepped down safely on the slippery floor.

I MENTION THE EVENT TO SHOW WHAT WAS DESTROYED. THIS man grew up in extreme poverty, won a scholarship to Tufts, got a degree in civil engineering, and then joined the army to become a lieutenant in the field artillery and fight in France during World War I. After the war, he designed and helped to build many of the subway tunnels in New York and Boston. Then he started Raytheon, a highly successful and now international company that made the radar we used in World War II.

After he retired as the CEO, he took us to the Kalahari Desert in what is now Namibia, where we made our lengthy study of the precontact San in an unmapped area of 120,000 square miles, a vast savanna-desert with no surface water.

If things had gone wrong, no one could help us or even find us. But thanks to my dad's foresight and planning, nothing even remotely bad happened to any of us. The San gave us water from their water holes, and my dad was a dead shot with a rifle. He'd see an antelope in the far distance, aim the rifle, pull the trigger, and the antelope would drop. Normally we ate canned food, but if by any chance we ran out of it, for as long as he had bullets, we'd have meat.

MY FASCINATION WITH THE NATURAL WORLD BEGAN WITH HIM. When my brother and I were children, he took us for walks in the woods around the home he had provided for us in New Hampshire, where we learned not only the tracks of animals and the names of trees but also how to start a fire with one match even if it's raining, what to do if we got lost, and how to find which way is south. If you're on standard time and point the hour hand of your watch at the sun, halfway between there and twelve is south.

I am who I am because of him. When we lost him, we lost our leader, the smartest, strongest, most capable person we had ever known. He died in a hospital with my mother, my daughter, and me beside him, quietly telling him how much we loved him, stroking his forehead, holding his hand.

Because I've never been able to cry as a grown-up, I didn't cry then. I doubt that this is good. Tears of grief are said to be different from the tears you shed when your eyes water. Tears of grief are said to contain a poison that crying removes from your brain. I must have been filled with that poison; of the five stages of grief we're said to have, I had just one of them—anger.

My wonderful father died on the night of the presidential election while a nearby television was blaring the news of Ronald Reagan's victory. *Good thing he can't hear this*, I thought.

After a while a young doctor who seemed happy, perhaps because of Reagan's victory, came bouncing in, raised both hands in the air, made little quotation marks with his fingers, and "pronounced" him dead. *Like you give a fuck, you asshole. You think he's dead because you say so? We know he's dead*, I thought.

MY MOTHER DIED IN 2002, TWO MONTHS BEFORE HER BIRTHDAY. I was seventy-one and she would have been 104. By then she was living with me in New Hampshire, and she died with me beside her.

It was just before dawn. The sky was turning gray, and coyotes in the nearby woods were singing. My mother seemed unconscious. She took a breath, waited for a while, took another soft breath, and was gone.

She was modest and endlessly gracious all her life. She was also productive. During her sixties and early seventies, she published a number of scholarly papers about the San she had studied while she was in her fifties. In 1976 when she was seventy-eight, she published her first book about the San, *The !Kung of Nyae Nyae*, with Harvard University Press. In 1999, when she was 101, she published her second book about the San, *Nyae Nyae !Kung Beliefs and Rites*, with Peabody Museum Press, also at Harvard.

By then she was living with me, so we went to the party given by the press to celebrate its publication. She had a nice time at the party. My mind's eye still sees her smiling, but by then she'd been experiencing memory loss and some confusion. Writers should hold the copyrights of their work, and she held the copyright of her first book. But the copyright of her second book, as I learned much later, is held by the president and fellows of Harvard College. Her confusion had begun by then, so I think she didn't know this, and neither did I when we were at the party.

The president and fellows of Harvard College had nothing to do with that book, and I see no reason for them to hold the copyright. Did they take it because she was old and experiencing some confusion? I would have made sure she held the copyright. As far as I know, she doesn't get the royalties. Maybe there aren't any royalties, or maybe the president and fellows of Harvard College are dining out on them.

NOT LONG AFTER THE PUBLICATION PARTY, A FRIEND CAME TO VISIT her. During the visit she politely asked him, "What are your plans for the summer?" He planned to climb Denali, formerly known as Mount McKinley, and was glad to describe the avalanches and crevasses he would need to avoid. This took a few minutes. My mother listened intently, looking at his face and smiling politely, until he finished his description and was expecting a response. My mother's mind was weakened, but her graciousness was strong. "What are your plans for the summer?" she asked.

HERE AGAIN I TELL OF DEMENTIA TO SHOW WHAT WAS LOST. LIKE my father, my mother was an only child, born in Arizona before it was a state. Her father oversaw the Morenci copper mine, but later he moved his family to California, where he worked in the company's management department until he died in an accident when my mom was seven or eight. She and her mother, my Gran, were left alone—their relatives were in Nova Scotia—but my mom went to the University of California at Berkeley, where she not only got her degree but also became a performing ballerina.

After she graduated, she and Gran traveled around the world, and when they returned, they found an apartment in South Hadley, Massachusetts, where my mom taught English literature at Mount Holyoke College, a job she'd learned about in China, where she met two Mount Holyoke professors who also were traveling. They liked her (who didn't?) and arranged for her to get the job. She and Gran were still together when my mom married my dad, and they all moved to Cambridge to be near the company he founded.

While in Cambridge, she got an MA in English literature from Radcliffe. And here I notice an interesting twist about a formal education. She had an MA in English lit and had taught it at Mount Holyoke, yet the great work she'd done in her study of the San had nothing to do with English lit; and even when she was in her forties she read nothing for entertainment except detective novels like *Murders in the Rue Morgue* and *The Hound of the Baskervilles*. (She'd probably already read the high-class stuff.)

Among her friends was Odile Sweeney, an accomplished African American woman, one of the directors of the YWCA, who lived in one of Cambridge's African American communities. At the community center, these two friends started a nonprofit workplace for the neighborhood women, where they salvaged tungsten from radio tubes produced by Raytheon if the tubes were found to be defective. The women could come whenever they liked, work for as long as they liked, and bring their children with them. The children were cared for by a volunteer who often enough was me. We had our own room with toys and children's books, and we played games and drew pictures. All the money went to the workers, and the project was highly successful.

Later, when my mom was in her fifties and we went to the Kalahari, although she'd had no formal training as an anthropologist, she became one when she was the first to study pre-contact hunter-gatherers with no contamination from the so-called civilized world. She said her life began at fifty.

For the books and academic papers she wrote about the San, she was awarded an honorary degree by the University of Toronto in Canada, and another by the University of Witwatersrand in Johannesburg, South Africa. The latter took place on April 13, 1994, and on April 27, apartheid officially ended in South Africa. Thus the award seemed exceptionally important, given to a woman whose work showed deep respect for African people.

To her, everyone was a valued, important individual. Age, gender, social class, religion, race, ethnicity, political affiliation, sexual orientation, financial status, country of origin, and achievement or lack of it were nothing to her. This may explain her success as an anthropologist, because in those days white people in what is now Namibia saw the San as animals and hunted them for sport along with other wildlife. My mother saw them as valued colleagues.

She gave money to the homeless when she saw them on the street, not as if she were some saintly benefactor, but more like a grateful customer happy to pay for some service. She was as respectful to them as she was to the high-ranking artists and academics who entered her life. Most of her charitable contributions were for the homeless.

Everyone loved her, several people named their daughters for her, and I wish I could say I took after her. Nobody thought I was like her—I smoked and swore and was called "unconventional"—but her friends would often console me, saying she was a hard act to follow. But was she? She didn't seem like a hard act—she seemed like a caring, intelligent leader, a pleasure and a privilege to follow.

From her I got my love of animals, so I took after her there, but love of animals isn't a virtue and I get no recognition for the resemblance. However, like her, I adopt homeless dogs and cats, feed birds and squirrels, and instead of killing the flies I find in the house, I take them outdoors to let them fly free. (She kept spiders because they're helpful, and I keep spiders too.)

My mother was softer than I am, though. When a bear was injured by a truck near my house and a police officer came to shoot him, I saved him by loudly informing the officer that he couldn't set foot on my land. "Go find a judge," I told him. "Get a search warrant!" The officer left in disgust, and the bear got better. He lived for many more years. I saw him often.

I doubt that my mother would have raised her voice when speaking to a police officer, nor would she have ordered him off her property. She would have tried politely to persuade him, but if he hadn't been persuaded, he would have shot the bear.

DID HER DEATH CHANGE ME? OF COURSE IT DID, BUT AGAIN IN AN interior fashion. On the day she died, I went on doing what I usually did, not crying because crying isn't in me. But I miss her painfully and think about her constantly, wondering what she'd say about whatever is happening. It's weird to live without your mother. My mother never got over the death of her mother. You're never the same.

MY BROTHER WAS SEVENTY-THREE AND I WAS SEVENTY-FOUR when he died of cancer. That happened in 2005, in a Boston hospital. For several days he was heavily sedated but still alive, so his wife and two stepsons stayed beside him during the day and I stayed beside him at night, driving from New Hampshire in the evening and going home in the morning when his wife and her sons arrived. They had beautiful music playing softly in his room. Despite the morphine, he could hear it, I believe.

He seemed to be in the hospice area of that hospital, because almost every night someone in one of the other rooms died. Most of them died alone, connected to monitors that buzzed in the nurses' station, and a nurse would hurry to the room.

If you're in a hospital, it's best to die during visiting hours. As far as I know, in perhaps eight rooms of the hospice area, only one other person spent nights with a dying patient. Loneliness can cause painful distress to the dying. We want to matter to someone and may suffer bitterly if we die alone.

The nurses knew this and felt pity for those people. While I was there, the man in the next room died alone, and the nurse who pronounced him was shaking her head in disapproval as she left his room. I also was sorry for those people and grateful that this wouldn't happen to my brother. He died in midmorning, his family at his side. I was deeply saddened and depressed, but our ways had parted long before this, and although I loved him dearly, his was yet another death that didn't change my world.

WITH THAT, MY BIRTH FAMILY WAS GONE. I HAD MY OWN FAMily, of course, and although I grieved for the others and missed them, my life went on as before. For a death to change this, at least in my case, the deceased had to be not only important to me, but important in a constant, intimate way.

This makes sense, if you think about it. The loss of a much-loved person leaves a deep wound in your heart, an empty space in your life that you'll never fill again, but you go on as before. The usual responsibilities surround you, so you don't have a choice.

But if your hand is cut off, you can't go on as before. You need your hand in a way you don't need another person. Its absence dominates your life because you miss it constantly, continuously, every minute, all the time.

I learned this from a dog, an Australian shepherd whose name was Pearl. When I met her, she belonged to my son's family, who at the time lived in Colorado, and although she liked her owners, when I came for a visit, she chose me to be her person. She'd spend the days beside me and sleep on my bed, pressed against me. We liked each other so much they gave us to each other.

After that, we did everything together. When I went shopping she'd wait in the car, watching for me out the window. When I took a shower, she'd wait by the shower curtain. If I was looking for one of our cats, she'd find him for me. If she barked at night, I'd get out of bed and look out the window, sure she knew something I didn't. Sometimes she'd scented the bear I saved. I was always glad to see him.

We absorbed each other and understood each other deeply, in a way we wouldn't have if both of us were human. If you're sick or depressed when someone asks how you're doing, you smile and say you're doing fine. Only your dog knows you're lying.

ONCE I HAD TO DO A BOOK SIGNING IN PROVIDENCE, RHODE IS-land. I've written about this in another book, but it's so important I must write about it twice. Pearl and I went together but arrived a bit late. I looked frantically for a parking place, which took forever, and then found one at last but couldn't find the bookstore. Pearl, on her leash, trotted patiently beside me as we ran around the streets. After I found the store and began to sign books, she hid under the counter to avoid the strangers who wanted to pat her. So she was glad when the event was over and we were out on the sidewalk, ready to go home.

But where was the car? Not only had I forgotten where I'd parked, I'd been so nervous because I was late that I didn't notice the name of the street! Providence has hundreds of streets with millions of cars parked on both sides. As I was wondering what in the world I could do about this, Pearl on her leash began to pull me. Since I could think of no other plan, I started walking.

For the longest time we walked, crossing streets and following sidewalks, going northwest in a fairly straight line. It couldn't have been the zigzag route we'd taken to the bookstore, so I thought we might be walking to New Hampshire. But suddenly Pearl pulled me off the sidewalk to walk a few feet up a street, where she stopped and looked up at me. I was puzzled—we'd come all the way on the sidewalks—until I saw that Pearl not only understood the problem but had solved it. I was standing by the left front door of my car.

Pearl normally got in through the rear doors. She'd brought me to the driver's door and was looking at me with a steady, serious expression. I think she was saying, *Get in*.

As we drove, she kept looking at me strangely. I believe my

incompetence surprised her. She may have wondered if she'd be required to show me how to get home.

SHE DIED IN 2010, EUTHANIZED BECAUSE OF INCURABLE CANCER. Not a day passes that I don't remember her beside me, looking trustfully and lovingly into my eyes as the poisoned needle pierced her skin.

I think about her all the time. I say her name when I'm alone. I dedicated one of my books to her. She seemed like a physical part of me, as if we shared one body. Now I blunder along as usual, but I'll never be the same. Did I say I never cry? I didn't when I left her still warm body at the veterinarian's to be cremated later, but I feel tears almost coming as I write this. That often happens when I think about her. Her death changed my life like no other. It may seem wrong or at best unusual to feel this way about a dog but not always to feel this way about a person. We can change how we act, but we can't change how we feel, and I know that I'll miss her forever. The people I loved and lost were other people, but Pearl was like my hand.

MY HUSBAND DIED IN 2015. HIS NAME WAS STEVE, AND WE BOTH were eighty-three. When he died of ALS, we'd been married for sixty years.

We met in 1950 when we were eighteen. He was a friend of my brother's, and we all were in college together. I was impressed with Steve. He had a marvelous sense of humor and a motorcycle he bought for himself by working on construction projects in the summers. He was impressed with me because, as he told me years later, I had a nice ass.

Annoyed as I was by his remark—I thought he'd liked my character—when looking back, it seems amazing that one person's motorcycle and another person's ass produced a long, loving sixty-year marriage. But that's young people for you—they have no idea what they're doing or getting themselves into. But we were lucky, and it worked for us. A friend said our marriage was successful because an ass joins a motorcycle when someone takes a ride.

Our journey lasted longer than many. In those days, and certainly in our parents' days, people understood "until death do us part" more clearly than they do now. Also, we were content to let each other lead the lives we chose, even though these were far from the same. Steve didn't mind when I took our little children to the wilds of northern Uganda with lions, leopards, and warlike pastoralists. He also didn't mind when I left the little children with him so I could spend a summer with wolves on Baffin Island.

And I didn't mind that Steve spent most of his time traveling around the country, assessing the electability of various senate candidates. He did this for the Council for a Liveable[*]

---

[*] "Liveable" is the way this name was spelled. Maybe the people who named it misspelled it. Don't look at me.

World, an organization that helped to finance the campaigns of senators in favor of reducing and eventually eliminating the US arsenal of nuclear weapons. At one time, thanks to him, half the people in the senate had been helped by the Council. I missed him, of course, but his work was important, and I thought he should do what he wanted, so when he was away we talked on the phone.

Nor did I mind years later when Steve, having retired from the Council, would spend six months of every year in the Czech Republic—three months in Prague, three months at home. In Prague, he pursued the subject of his graduate studies, the history of central Europe, by researching the ethnic conflict that prevailed in Czechoslovakia after World War I. He spoke six languages and was fluent in Czech, Russian, and German, so he was well prepared, but he couldn't have done this earlier, because Czechoslovakia was behind the Iron Curtain until 1991 and the archives were closed to people from non-Communist countries. I missed him when he was in Prague, although I'd visit him, but he loved what he was doing, so I didn't complain.

We fought, of course—as far as I know, most married people fight, although my parents didn't, or not loudly—and at one time I thought of getting a divorce but not without doubts. I remembered my friend's image of bonding with a motorcycle and also a message I'd seen on a biker's T-shirt: "If you can read this, the bitch fell off."

So when I went to the office of a lawyer friend to see about divorcing, I was shaking so hard I could barely speak. My lawyer friend got worried and told me to think it over. I apologized for taking his time and went home.

Steve wouldn't discuss divorce. The main reason he was angry with me was because I'd been considering it. So even though we'd been getting along poorly, we wanted to resolve our differences—I can't remember what they were—and spend the rest of our lives together, so we did. We just forgot whatever it was we'd been fighting about and slid back into being one person.

For many years now, I've had the same license plate. It's STET, which is his initials and mine. Evidently it comes from the Latin verb *sto, stare, steti, statum*, meaning "let it stand," and, as I've mentioned earlier, if an editor has changed something a writer has written, it's the writer's way of saying, "Don't change this."

Love is one thing when you fall in it, because this involves yourself and another person who is clearly someone else. It's quite another thing after you've joined so tightly that you might as well be one person.

THE ONLY TIME I EVER CRIED AS AN ADULT WAS WHEN A DOCTOR told Steve that the life expectancy of someone with ALS is three to five years after diagnosis. The name—amyotrophic lateral sclerosis—means "no muscle nourishment." The disease destroys your nerves, and there is no cure or treatment, but Steve accepted the news without changing his facial expression. The doctor might have said we were having fine weather.

But I was so shocked I burst into tears and cried out loud, choking, sobbing, tears pouring. Steve's expression changed from calmness to concern. With difficulty, because the ALS had started in his feet and the muscles there were quitting, he made his way across the room to put his arms around me. He had caused me to cry. He stroked my hair and apologized for dying. "I'm *so* sorry," he said softly.

Did his death change my life? That's when I first felt myself aging. I was always tired. I couldn't pay attention. I felt lost. Did death seem good because he was dead, and when I was dead we'd be together? It seemed I couldn't get there fast enough. As I remember, I felt myself aging even before the memorial service. I forgot where the post office was and had to try a few times before I found it. I lost my wristwatch, had to buy a new one, and then found the lost one at the back of my desk.

As time went by, my aging got worse. I'd lose my glasses. Sometimes they'd be up on my head as I was searching the house and my office for them, but not always, and once a whole week passed and still I couldn't find them. That made life difficult, as I couldn't see well without them and was relying on an old pair I'd replaced about fifteen years before. I almost fell headlong down a flight of stairs because I couldn't distinguish the step I was on from the step below it.

This couldn't continue, so I bought a new pair of glasses (very expensive), and wouldn't you know? The very next day, my dear friend Jan, who now helps me with the housework, found the lost ones.

Almost every day I'd lose my car key. *Gosh, my car is on the driveway, so the key must be here. Did I leave it in the car? Was it in my hand when I hung up my coat?* Do you see what the last question says? It says, *The key is in your coat pocket*, but my mind had stopped working like that. I remembered something a psychiatrist friend once told me: it doesn't matter if you forget where something is, as long as you remember what it's for. If I couldn't remember what the key was for, I wouldn't be trying to find it, so I found this helpful. And it *was* in my coat pocket—I found it a year later when I put on the coat. But I lost it again. It must be in the house, because again the car was in the driveway, but again a year has almost passed, and I still haven't found it. Luckily, I had two keys. The spare key is now on a big yellow wristband, so it shows up when it's somewhere it shouldn't be.

I FORGOT HOW TO COOK. I WAS A GOOD COOK, ACCORDING TO Steve. I cooked for him, but the only thing cooking does for me now is tell me I'm the only one who's going to eat this mess. I go to bed early because I've nothing better to do, and I wake up around four in the morning, always depressed. So I turn on the lights and the television, which helps because the news is often depressing enough to overcome my personal depression. Then

I feed the dogs and cats, drink a little coffee, and go back to work. I brighten when I'm working.

My experience with my husband's death seemed unique, at least to me, but in fact it is common. Millions of us have long, loving marriages in which the two become one person. If one of us dies, this is what happens to the half that remains.

NOT LONG AGO I WAS TALKING WITH MY GRANDSON NAMPAL. HE was twelve at the time, and he and his parents—my son and his wife—live across the road. I think we were talking about what would happen to my house when I die—that his father (my son) and his aunt (my daughter) would inherit it—and I was surprised to see the horror on his face. His young eyes filled with tears and he reached his arms toward me. "You can't die," he said.

"But everyone dies," I told him.

"Not you," he said.

I told him I was still in good health and would surely live much longer. He looked slightly relieved, as if I'd changed the subject, and again it came to me that death has different meanings depending on your age. Young people seldom consider the terrible things of the future; they haven't lived long enough to have informational pasts, so they see things differently than we elders do. I remembered myself looking up at the shower faucet, having just heard that someone had died. Nampal was doing what I had done, which was to view death as shocking or abnormal. Young people lack the concerns of their elders and have a different set of fears. Grandchildren give you perspective.

I OFTEN HAVE DINNER WITH NAMPAL'S FAMILY, BUT NOT LONG after our discussion his parents went out for the evening and he had dinner with me. Since I'd forgotten how to cook, we ordered a pizza, drove to town and got it, and then drove back to my house and ate it while watching a TV program made by the people who make *The Simpsons*. Nampal chose the program, and because I'm forgetful, I don't remember what it was called, but it was excellent.

I seldom laugh out loud, and, except for the time I learned you live three to five years after being diagnosed with ALS, I never cry. But being with a young person can change you. Sometimes you feel young too, as I did that evening, so I did both. I laughed so hard I cried because the program was so funny, and I'm hoping we do that again.

A few days later, I felt so grateful that I gave Nampal my most treasured object, a cast of the skull of a saber-tooth tiger. It's huge. Nampal was ecstatic. He says it's his favorite possession.

No doubt the science-minded will want to know the species, and I'm pleased to say it was a *Smilodon fatalis*, subspecies *californicus*, who, maybe thirty thousand years ago, died in the La Brea tar pits. These are in a run-down section of Los Angeles where saber-tooth tigers once lived.

Fourteen

This chapter is about death itself. Not that it's a great subject, but all of us die, so it's good to be prepared. It's simple enough if we're the ones who die, but our death can cause problems for those who are left with the body and must do something about it. The method we choose depends on our culture, and worldwide there seem to be six. These, in order of their appearance, are exposure, burial, cannibalism, cremation, liquefaction, and human composting.

The first, of course, is exposure, practiced by our hominid ancestors, who did what other species did—when one of them died, the others, however saddened, would leave the body to become a meal for scavengers ranging from ants to vultures and hyenas.

The concept of burial may have appeared because our ancestors came to realize that we have spirits, if in fact we do. And because a spirit is not visible, has no odor, and makes no sounds, it's like an idea. To communicate a complicated idea with nothing graphic present is not possible for other animals, so surely the belief arose after we developed language.

A grave, in a way, is the acknowledgment of a spirit, and in the past as well as today the cultures that use graves acknowledge spirits.

FOR MOST OF OUR HISTORY AS A SPECIES, BURIALS WERE THE norm. We keep the early tradition to this day with green burial or natural burial, in which the body is not embalmed and is placed very simply in a fairly shallow grave. Today, the body may or may not be in a plain wooden coffin, but that's essentially the only difference; thus the method in use in the earliest times is with us still.

The earliest known burial was that of a Neandertal man, buried 130,000 years ago. The horn of an aurochs—an extinct species of wild cattle—was in the grave with him. What's said to be the earliest known burial of our species took place near what now is Israel—a woman and a child, buried 100,000 years ago. It's said to be the first for our species, but almost surely it wasn't. We humans lived in Africa for thousands of years before going to the Middle East, and for much of that time our Khoisan ancestors (Khoisan is the name for the San and the Khoikhoi* people combined) almost certainly buried their dead.

Their culture was ancient and very stable. I've mentioned an occupied San encampment where people had lived continuously for 85,000 years, during which the material culture remained essentially unchanged. These people must have buried their dead, but I know of no fossils—few fossils of any kind are found in that area, probably due to the dry, sandy condition of the earth and the shallowness of the graves. In many soil conditions, not just this kind, the person in the grave would be unlikely to become a fossil.

Could graves have begun with *Homo erectus*, who gave rise to us and also to Neandertals? If *Homo erectus* invented graves, the graves might well have been like those of the San, as there aren't many other possibilities.

SAN GRAVES VARIED SOMEWHAT. AS MY MOTHER WROTE IN *NYAE Nyae !Kung Beliefs and Rites*, "The ideal grave is deep enough to receive a flexed body. Ideal graves, however, are not always achieved; a shallow trench-shaped grave might be made instead. It might be very shallow, more a symbol of a grave than an actual excavation, or, without even a symbol of a grave,

---

* The Khoikhoi—people very like the San—were pejoratively known as Hottentots.

the body might be stretched out on the ground and covered with thorny branches to protect it from the carnivores."* This might be the case if the people were traveling when someone died. The Nyae Nyae area had no surface water. In the dry season, the people's destination could be a distant water hole; they'd carry just enough water to make the trip, and they'd need to be on their way.

After a burial, people stayed away from the grave. If they stayed nearby, the spirit might become displeased and do something to harm them. Considering the steady, ongoing culture of the San, we might safely assume that a belief in spirits was involved with the existence of graves.

TO ASSUME THAT GRAVES IN THE MIDDLE EAST PRECEDED THE graves of the San is the result of inadequate evidence. But this doesn't mean that Neandertals weren't the first hominins to have graves, or that the Khoisan weren't the first of our species to make them. What it means is that green burial, or natural burial, has been with us for many thousands of years and is ongoing. It also means that exposure and burial were by far the most common methods of handling the dead. We still use green burial—it's legal in all fifty states, perhaps with different regulations, but legal just the same. One wonders if these will leave fossils.

---

* Marshall, Lorna J. *Nyae Nyae !Kung Beliefs and Rites*, p. 181.

But what I would call "regular burial" has changed greatly. One thing that hasn't changed, however, and has appeared worldwide, is a sense that the dead know what we're doing. Their survivors put objects in the graves for them to enjoy or use later. For all we know, the Neandertal mentioned earlier had a spirit and so did the aurochs whose horn was in with him. Some cultures put objects in graves and others don't. We do, the Neandertals did, the San don't.

THE DODOTH I VISITED IN NORTHERN UGANDA PRACTICED BURIAL *and* exposure. The Dodoth were a pastoral people who favored cattle above all else, and important men were buried in their cattle pens. The bodies of most other people were exposed.

I happened to see the exposed body of a man who had just been killed. I knew his sister. Her name was Adwong, and we were good friends, but I'd never met her brother, who was known for robbing people. He was killed while trying to rob a granary; the owner, who also knew him, speared him in the abdomen. His body was perhaps a hundred feet from the owner's compound, so he must have turned to run away after he was speared.

He also must have suffered. He was lying on his back with his face somewhat constricted, as if he'd died in pain. His abdomen was cut almost from his chest to his hips, most of his intestines had spilled out, and hundreds of ants had found them. My guess is that ants are the first to scavenge an exposed body.

Standing with others as we looked at Adwong's brother, I wondered aloud what would happen to his body. "Hyenas," someone said. And yes, that night hyenas found him. This was what everyone expected. In the Dodoth area, hyenas almost always appeared soon after a corpse was exposed. Hyenas weren't hated, feared, or hunted, although they were associated with death in several ways. For instance, it was said that witches rode on hyenas to circle the compounds of those they were trying to harm. But even though hyenas had a shady reputation, they were helpful. They were the undertakers.

AS FOR AN HONORED ELDER WHO DIED, A GRAVE WOULD BE DUG IN his cattle pen while his cattle were out grazing. His body would be lowered respectfully into the grave, which would then be filled and closed, and his cattle would return in the evening. If I were a pastoralist, this would be a form of heaven—my cattle around me at night like a beautiful dream. Who could ask for more? (Alas, I couldn't ask. I'm a woman, and even if I were a man, I wouldn't be sufficiently important.)

CANNIBALISM APPEARED IN EARLY TIMES. I PUT IT IN THIRD place when listing ways of handling the dead, as if it were the third method to appear, but it could be almost anywhere on the list except toward the end, because nobody knows when it began. Sometimes our primate relatives eat others of their kind, or at least take bites out of them, and even after we came down from the trees, it's hard to imagine we didn't do the same.

Today, cannibalism has different purposes in various cultures. In some it's a sacred practice, as it was in various cultures long ago. A certain cave in England showed possible ritualistic cannibalism that occurred about 15,000 years ago. In other cultures, it's a way to strengthen people. In modern times some African child soldiers were asked to eat the dead as part of a strengthening initiation ritual. Evidently in some cultures it's for gourmet purposes. I'm told that China once had recipes for preparing human flesh.

And sometimes it's from necessity, as it was for the Donner party, a group of Americans in 1846 heading west with a wagon train that was stopped by massive blizzards in the Sierra mountains. After the people had eaten the oxen who pulled their wagons, they had no other food. Almost half of them died of starvation. Some of those who survived ate those who had already died.

ABOVE ARE SOME OF THE REASONS FOR CANNIBALISM, BUT HERE I'll limit this report to cultures where the purpose of cannibalism is the same as the purpose of burial and cremation—a way of protecting the dead. In this context, the intention is to

ELIZABETH MARSHALL THOMAS

help the soul or the essence of the deceased by moving it into a living body.

For example, the Aghori monks of India practice cannibalism, which gave rise to disgusting stories about them, claiming that Aghoris hung around cemeteries in hope of a good meal. These claims conflict sharply with more responsible reports* that show Aghori cannibalism to be sacred, performed to save the deceased from an undesirable reincarnation. If a soul is not inside a living person, it might return inside an insect or a frog. For the Aghori, cannibalism also facilitates bonding. A spiritual Aghori leader on the verge of death offered his flesh to a young ascetic as a blessing that would bond them.†

Cannibalism was seen in Paraguay among the Guayaki or Aché people, and here again the purpose was to place the soul inside a living person. Like the Aghori in India, these people wanted their souls to remain among the living.

Most of us in Western cultures see cannibalism as just about the worst thing we can imagine. We don't take into account its purpose in the cultures where it's meant to help the dead, to save the spirit, to join people together.

Nor do we take into account that many of us arrive at this notion ourselves. An American friend of mine, a delicate, sensitive woman, tells me that as her father was dying, she thought

---

* Trupal Pandya, "Aghori: The Holy Men," www.trupalpandya.com/blog/2017/4/13/aghori-the-holy-men.
† Ron Barrett, *Aghor Medicine: Pollution, Death, and Healing in Northern India* (Berkeley and Los Angeles: Univ. of California Press, 2008).

164

of eating him, to have him inside herself, to keep him. A friend of hers thought the same thing about her mother as she saw her in her coffin, about to be taken from her. A dear friend of mine lost her son to AIDS, and we went together to scatter his ashes in the sea by a beach he had loved. Before we scattered the ashes, my friend licked her finger, put it in the urn, collected some ashes on her finger, and put them in her mouth. She put her son inside her.

In a way, we all want to keep our loved ones inside us. When I was falling asleep and heard my grandmother say "Elizabeth," although she'd been dead for almost thirty years, she was inside me. Most of us feel that the dead live inside us, in our hearts.

CREMATION APPEARED AT DIFFERENT TIMES IN DIFFERENT places, and the cultures that practiced it didn't necessarily learn from one another. The first known cremation took place in Australia about 4,000 years ago, and later it was practiced intermittently throughout the Middle East, but then became forbidden in many Middle Eastern cultures. Judaism forbids cremation, for instance; it vehemently did so in the past, although now the prohibition may be lifting.

Christians also forbade cremation. Christianity pictures a specific afterlife in which your body itself goes to heaven or hell. And what if you went to hell? How would the Devil feel if ashes arrived? He couldn't torture them.

Some people, such as the Romans, practiced both burial and cremation, burying some and cremating others. The upper classes were cremated and the peasants were buried, as burial was considered a primitive custom, thus appropriate for the lower classes. The Greeks practiced both at the same time, cremating a body and burying the ashes in a container such as an urn.

Hindu culture valued cremation highly, and many cremations took place along the Ganges River. Today, burning ghats—crematoriums—are built on the banks of that river, and the ashes are placed in the river, from which the spirit goes to the sky. This resembles the Christian concept of eternal life, because the spirits remain there forever. It's another method of avoiding reincarnation.

In parts of Europe, England in particular, people were burned at the stake as punishment, and perhaps because of this, the practice of cremation moved slowly and wasn't generally accepted. One advocate for cremation said it would prevent premature burials, which sounds kind of spooky. Isn't a premature burial better than a premature cremation?

What seems to have promoted cremation in parts of Europe was the growing population and the increasing number of people who were dying. Because the ground became polluted by a burial and more polluted by many burials, cremation was suggested as the road to sanitation and public health. The concept wasn't accepted quickly, although some deceased people were cremated illegally, but at last it was accepted and the first legal cremation took place in 1885.

At about this time, people in the United States began to consider cremation. The Catholic Church banned it, but some Protestant churches accepted it, based on the theory that God can do whatever he wants and can resurrect those who were cremated. Catholics were more skeptical, but in 1963 Pope Paul VI lifted the ban. Today in the United States cremation is legal everywhere and is gaining popularity. In 2018 it was predicted that by 2020, more than half of the deceased will have chosen cremation.

We've come a long way from the days of exposure and the quiet simplicity of natural burial. Exposure disappeared in all but a few cultures, at least as a norm, and was replaced mostly by burial, which now is being surpassed by cremation, at least in some countries.

And again we're moving forward by inventing something new. The new method has several names, one of which is liquefaction. It's been in use for other disposals—it was used to decompose cattle with mad-cow disease as a way of preventing the spread of the infection—and now we're considering it for ourselves. On the internet I found a site called "An Alternative to Burial and Cremation Gains Popularity," and here's the introduction: "Fifteen states, most recently California, have rules allowing for the liquefaction of human remains through a process called alkaline hydrolysis."

What is alkaline hydrolysis? In alkaline hydrolysis a body is placed in a large pressurized vessel, water and potassium hydroxide are added, and the vessel is heated to 300°F for about three hours. By then, everything except the bones has turned to liquid, and the bones are soft. These are collected and crushed into dust, which, like the ashes of cremation, is given to the person's family. And as the smoke from cremation goes up the chimney, so liquefied remains go down the drain.

That the molecules of our bodies are in smoke going up to the sky seems agreeable. But the image of our molecules as a liquid going down to a sewer with everything else that goes there might lack appeal. I imagine myself on my way to the sewer just as a neighbor flushes a toilet he has filled with diarrhea. And what about pollution? Juice that dissolves a human body could be a serious pollutant, and it doesn't stay in the sewer. It leaks out.

A POSSIBLE RATIONALIZATION FOR LIQUEFACTION COULD BE THAT, along with cremation, it's less expensive than a fancy burial. At least at one facility the cost was between $1,800 and $3,000, which, if typical, puts the process fairly level with cremation.

This has been noticed. With cremation gaining popularity, promoters of liquefaction now call it hydro cremation. Reality can be discouraging, and when something we want to sell might seem disgusting, we give it a name that makes it seem natural and professional. Even so, to join "water" with "cremation" seems unusual. We all know that "hydro" means "water," but "cremation" comes from the Latin *cremare*, which, plain and simple, means "to burn." If there's one thing that doesn't burn, it's water, so this is a bit like calling a horse a "cat" and pretending you know what you're doing.

But who knows? Cremation was feared and considered disgusting but now is becoming popular, not only because it costs less than a regular funeral, but also because the cemeteries are getting full. Also, to burn a loved one may seem less attractive than dissolving him or her in water. So one of these days liquefaction, more pleasantly known as hydro cremation, might seem like an excellent choice to many, if not to me.

Even liquefaction may soon be overtaken, this time by something I'd like for myself. Green burial has inspired what might be seen as the sixth, most modern method of handling a corpse, or what might also be seen as the earliest and simplest method—a process that's expected to become legal in May 2020, at least in Washington State. It's called "natural organic reduction," or "human composting," and it involves straw, alfalfa, some wood chips, and the normal microbes that live in the soil and do the work. All of these items will be packed in a large box with the body, and a month or two later, a cubic yard of compost will result. You can use it in your garden or for your houseplants because it's the same as the topsoil you buy in a bag from a store.

It will be offered by a company called Recompose, based in Seattle and founded by Katrina Spade, and the cost for the process, which will include a funeral ceremony, will very likely be $5,500. Thus it will be a bit more expensive than cremation but less expensive than a regular funeral. It's by far the most environmentally friendly of all modern procedures, and in my view it's worth every dime.

Are we sure it will work? Of course it will work. The method is already in use for disposing of farm animals, but it's older than farm animals—it's been working every day, day after day, ever since death was invented, or at least since life arrived on land.

Fifteen

Today, the choice of posthumous disposal seems to be explained in part by money, which brings us to the question of the funeral. To honor the dead, many cultures have funerals, and in ours the outrageous fees charged by many funeral homes have been called the third greatest expense a family can encounter, after buying a house and a car.

The funeral industry denies this, but it's easily confirmed. At the time of this writing, the most expensive house in my area—Hillsboro County, New Hampshire—is about $700,000, although others have sold for much more. The average price of a new car might be between $25,000 and $30,000, and the price of an ordinary funeral could be upwards of $15,000, although the fancier funerals cost much more. Ronald Reagan's funeral cost $400 million.

The fanciest funerals involve parades and parties, but any funeral involves payment for a grave (unless you already have one), the funeral director's services, a coffin made of metal or mahogany and lined with plush, the embalming process, the grooming process that makes the dead person look like he or she is sleeping, and big bouquets of expensive flowers. Then there's rental of a viewing area where friends and family can see the well-dressed body, then the funeral service, then opening the grave, then renting a hearse to take the coffin to the cemetery and limousines to take the family to the cemetery, then closing the grave, obtaining a death certificate, and publishing an obituary, all with inflated prices.

For the source of much of this alarming information and to learn a lot more, you might want to read *The American Way of Death Revisited* by Jessica Mitford, an updated version of her game-changing bestseller, *The American Way of Death*, published in 1963. This is one of the most important books in recent history, as it exposes the funeral industry for mercilessly preying upon grieving families at their most vulnerable time. Not every funeral home is guilty of this behavior; some that aren't might be in rural communities and privately owned, not owned by one of the large funeral companies. But many are as described above.

MOST OF US DON'T KNOW WHAT FUNERALS INVOLVE. WHEN A family member dies, we suddenly transition from caring for a loved one to dealing with a body, and we turn to a funeral home where we've attended a funeral, or one that fits our religious beliefs, or one near where we live that we see as we drive by.

If we were buying a house or a car, we'd shop and compare prices, but we don't do this for funerals, because the death of a loved one is a serious matter that must be dealt with at once—an experience that is the direct opposite of buying something you want. When we choose a familiar funeral home, not knowing any better, we accept the conditions and do what we're told. And once the funeral is over, we have no reason to tell others about the expense, which we assume was normal, so we don't transmit what we've learned.

I don't want a funeral. Neither did my husband. I want to be cremated, just as he was. In my case, perhaps the best approach would be through the local cremation society, which does everything that's necessary for a reasonable price. This contrasts with the local funeral homes in our area, which arrange for cremation but charge twice as much; but even these are much less expensive than the outrageous ones described in *The American Way of Death* and its sequel.

We hadn't read these books at the time—my husband never read them, and I read them only because I was writing this book—but my husband already had bad feelings about funerals, and because he was the first of us to die, we did it his way.

If not for him, I would not have wanted to be cremated. It takes about an hour to cremate 100 pounds of human flesh and I weigh about 130 pounds, which would take about an hour and fifteen minutes. I imagined I might not be completely dead when pushed inside the furnace, and I'd wake up to find myself on fire. I imagined myself banging on the furnace wall and shouting, "Let me out!"

But then I learned about embalming, which seemed even worse. They put tubes in your veins and squirt toxic chemicals all through your body to wash out your blood. What if you woke up while that was happening? The chemicals stay inside you, allegedly to preserve you forever, or that's what you're supposed to believe—embalming is often called "eternal preservation"—but this is far from true. Even though you're embalmed, you decompose in time. By then you're in a coffin that might easily have cost upwards of $8,000 and is also decomposing down there in damp ground.

As for me, I assumed I'd have a regular funeral because everyone seems to—it's what you do. But that was when I feared cremation and knew nothing about embalming. Only when considering my husband's cremation did I learn that your body is kept for at least two days before they set you on fire. If you're really dead, your body will stiffen with rigor mortis within a few hours and lose the stiffness after two days.

Long before my husband died, he told me what he wanted, and I realized I wanted that too. It's certainly better than being in a coffin, because if I'm in a coffin I'll take up too much space in our grave site, and others might want to be buried there too.

At first, we planned to have our ashes scattered in the woods. But these days nothing is permanent—our ashes might find themselves under a pipeline or a highway. The cemetery is better. It's sanctified ground, so it can't be disturbed, our loved ones are in it, and our names are on the headstones. This doesn't mean there's anything wrong with scattering ashes—it just means we like that cemetery.

WHAT ABOUT GREEN BURIAL OR HUMAN COMPOSTING IF THE latter was available? These are good for many reasons as they involve no fossil fuel, no embalming, no vault, and no expensive casket. The natural processes are good for everyone, not only for the participants, the environment (cremation uses large amounts of fossil fuel), and the organisms that aid in decomposition, but also because they don't endanger the people who prepare the body. The toxic chemicals used by embalmers can give them cancer or ALS. Since human composting is not yet available in New Hampshire, I'd choose green burial and be in the field by my house, but those I love and want to be with are already in the cemetery.

THERE'S MUCH TO BE SAID ABOUT TRADITIONS FROM THE PAST, especially when it comes to death and dying. Most were

simple and peaceful. By far the most beautiful, most soothing experience with death I ever took part in was that of my
neighbor Lisa, who died after a long illness. Her body was
in a plain wooden coffin, and for several days and nights the
people who knew her and loved her took turns sitting beside
her. She was never alone.

Sy and I participated, sitting quietly with Lisa in a small
room, remembering her, thinking how much we would miss
her, hearing the voices of others who loved her—a deeply
peaceful, quiet experience, utterly personal, with none of the
stiffness and formality we might see in a regular funeral.

Later, I learned about doulas. As it happened, a friend named
Deana Darby was a doula, someone trained to help people during their two most important transitions, either when entering
life during birth or when leaving it in death. Deana would be
known as a death doula or a midwife to the dying, and she was
kind enough to tell me about the help she can give.

This is most needed when we transition from illness to
death, a process that may be hindered by our loved ones who
don't want us to leave them. This is natural and normal—they
want to remind us of what's happening around us or of the
good things we did together. They hold on to us as if begging
us to stay, which forces us to struggle. A doula helps them create an environment that supports our passage.

Deana cites ancient teachings that tell us we are a con-
glomeration of five elements—earth, air, space, fire, and
water—and we leave our world by dissolving into the lightest

of these, which is space. A doula can help a family support the process in various ways, one of which is by teaching them to match their breathing with ours. This can relax us, and let us breathe more and more slowly. Softly, we turn into space, our bodies empty, and we're gone.

I've imagined myself being cremated, being embalmed, and even being flushed down the sewer, and now I imagine myself breathing with others as I slowly turn into space. The breaths become fewer and smaller as the space grows bigger and wider. The breathing stops, and with it, my body, but the space that was me stays on.

As space, you last for three days. Some families have visiting periods that last for three days. The people who love you take turns sitting with you until three days have passed and the space that was you has vanished. What's left behind is just a body.

Wakes and visiting hours take many forms and have many explanations. I don't know about all of them, or if something like that was happening when Sy and I sat by Lisa in her coffin. I hope it was happening. It could have been happening.

WITHOUT A DOULA, THE EXPERIENCE OF DEATH CAN BE VERY DIF-ferent and seldom as good. A doula could have prevented the death of my husband from being a nightmare experience, perhaps for him, but certainly for me.

Steve was in a hospital, transitioning from life to death,

when we were given the choice of letting him go or keeping him alive. To keep him alive involved not only the various hospital devices attached to him at the time, but later would involve an oxygen tank in a heavy machine that he'd be attached to permanently.

His body had failed completely. He couldn't move, talk, eat, drink, or breathe on his own, and he'd never get better. Only his brain functioned well. That's why ALS is so terrible. We saw him imprisoned in a body kept alive by a machine that breathed for him but unable to communicate what his excellent brain was thinking. Knowing that for the rest of our lives we'd regret our decision but unaware of what would happen next, we painfully decided not to do this to him.

My memory of his death is as follows. Moments after we informed the doctor of our decision, we went to his room with two nurses right behind us. Cheerful, smiling, and talking to each other, they yanked out the devices that were keeping him alive. Did that wonderful mind of his know what was happening? As I remember, the nurses didn't check his heartbeat or his breathing as, I later learned, they should have done, but as they were leaving, one looked at us over her shoulder and brightly said, "He's dead." I guess this was the pronouncement. Then they hurried out the door.

Our son and daughter remember this differently. They tell me he didn't die quickly, and we were able to hold his hand and tell him we loved him. Perhaps they're right. All I remember is the horror. Or perhaps I'm right, and our son and daughter are remembering what happened *before* we consulted with the doctor. Before we did so, we were with Steve, telling him we loved him, holding his hand.

At least he was unconscious or almost unconscious when we killed him. The only consolation here is that his neurologist, whose patient he'd been since his diagnosis, told us that without a doubt we'd done the right thing. This may or may not be true—what else would she say about a done deal—although the idea is consoling. But we certainly didn't do it the right way, and that is far from consoling.

WHEN I THINK OF STEVE'S DEATH, I ALSO THINK OF THE DEATH of my longtime friend and assistant Bella, who was also very dear to me. The cancer had spread throughout her body. She was telling others it wouldn't be long and was transitioning when, at the very last minute, she asked for an ambulance, but not because she thought it would save her life. She may have decided not to die in the bed she shared with her husband, because the memory would sadden him when he was trying to sleep, or she may have wanted to spare her family from witnessing her death or dealing with her body. Perhaps she had all these reasons. The ambulance came, and she died on her way to the hospital.

Bella was heroic. She cared about others. But perhaps a doula could have convinced her that at a time like this, her interests were more important.

Another dear friend told me about the death of her father, also in a hospital. His experience seemed especially harsh, because he knew what was happening and struggled furiously to stay alive, coughing blood and gasping for air until he could gasp no longer.

A doula could have helped all three of these people. If they'd been quietly surrounded by those who loved them, with everyone knowing and accepting what was happening, they could have eased into space and died softly.

Sixteen

The treatment of dying patients matters greatly, and so does the treatment of their survivors. The person who died may be surrounded by family and friends who are trying to cope with what just happened, but the person must be legally pronounced dead, which can be done by a variety of people from a doctor or registered nurse to an EMT during an ambulance call. Normally it's done by a doctor or nurse if the person dies in a hospital and by the person's hospice nurse if the person dies at home.

This pronouncement can be rough if the death is in a hospital—witness my husband's and my father's. In my father's case, a tall young doctor burst into the room, looked at the machines that were attached to my dad, looked at us as if he was in a hurry, threw up his hands, said, "I pronounce him dead," then turned his back and left.

This doctor had relied on the machines and didn't feel my dad's wrist to make sure his heart had stopped, which probably he should have done, because sometimes the machines are mistaken. The internet abounds with stories of people who were wrongly pronounced, and my friend Nancy, a hospice nurse, tells me that indeed this does happen. The way to avoid it, she says, is to physically examine the person, not to rely on a machine. This means that an unknown number of people could have been wrongly pronounced. I didn't know this when Steve died. Perhaps he was wrongly pronounced.

HOSPICE NURSES PRONOUNCED MY MOTHER, WHICH THEY DID RE-spectfully and quietly, checking her breathing and her heart, but when they went to the adjoining bathroom to remove her medications from the cupboard, they were chatting and laughing like the nurses who removed the life-support devices from my husband.

I didn't know why my mother's nurses were emptying the cupboard, so they told me it was required. Later I learned that the process is to remove opioids, if any, because each pill is said to be worth $80 on the street, and the survivors might sell them. My mother had been experiencing a certain amount of pain for which some opioid had been prescribed, but the pills were in one small bottle, and the nurses took just about everything in the cupboard. This seemed callous and also rather needless, because if we had planned to sell the contents of the cupboard, we would have hidden them before the hospice nurses came. But I didn't care what they did. *Take her toothpaste if you want it*, I thought.

Even with inconsiderate pronouncers (who can be found anywhere), it's still best to die at home, certainly in our community. I've learned this from my friend Nancy, who in sharp contrast to the doctor and nurses described above, is a sensitive, thoughtful person who respects the families of the people she must pronounce.

When she finds herself in the bedroom of a patient who has just died and is surrounded by his family, she quietly explains what she must do and shows the family the printed copy of her orders. She asks them to help her. Thus the family members, not Nancy, are the ones who collect the opioids and other medicines. Nancy's procedure is not invasive, although she stays in the background to be sure it's done right.

Before this, she must pronounce her patient dead. She says that making a mistake is easy. She says the line between being alive and being dead is small, and you must be aware of all the signs. Nancy makes sure the person's pupils don't move if something passes over them. She makes sure the heartbeat has stopped, and the person isn't breathing. These observations must be done carefully, especially of the breathing, because while you transition, the breaths you take can be soft and far apart.

I once asked Nancy what were the best and worst things about being a hospice nurse. She said the worst thing is that she often sees so many patients a day that she must hurry from one to the next, unable to spend extra time with them after she's done the necessary procedures. She feels she can help them by learning their thoughts or just by giving them a chance to talk with someone who understands their situation, and if she must leave too soon, she disappoints them.

As for the best part, she can help her patients "write the script for the end of life," as she put it. Patients have more autonomy at home than they do in a hospital and can choose how to be handled. They can choose for the hospice nurse to visit every day or once a week. If they're not under serious therapy, they can choose to be lightly or heavily medicated. They can choose to go on a trip if they like. A hospital offers no such choices.

Nancy is sensitive to her patients' perceptions of death. She's seen that those with deep religious faith can accept death easily because they will be going to heaven. Those who have fulfilled their lives, are loved by good people, and have done everything they wanted to do can also accept death easily. But if a patient isn't ready or the family isn't ready—Nancy has been in homes where the family has forbidden the use of words like "die," "death," or "hospice"—the event will be difficult for everyone.

Nancy talks with the families of her patients, preparing

them for what will happen. The families thank her. Many want to stay in touch with her. Not long ago she got a letter from the family of a child who had been in her care and whose death was highly traumatic. But Nancy must have helped this family. A few months later they wrote to her, thanking her for her compassion and her gentle care. She had a special place in their hearts, they told her. When they ended the letter, instead of writing "Sincerely" or "Yours truly," they wrote "With respect."

Seventeen

Before you die, you should prepare. Your loved ones don't want to think about your death and may not be prepared, and in case this is true of my loved ones, I wrote a document stating my preferences. And rather than filing it somewhere, I'll stick it on the front of the refrigerator or perhaps on the kitchen wall. Everyone will see it, and unless they have a better idea, they'll know what to do when the time comes. The document follows.

1. First, I don't mind dying. Everybody does it, and I'll live in your hearts. But I'd rather die at home

if possible, not in a hospital. I want a hospice nurse as good as Nancy, but maybe someone other than Nancy—we're such good friends that having to pronounce me dead might distress her. I imagine myself being asked to pronounce her, which would certainly distress me.

Also, unless natural organic reduction—the process mentioned earlier that turns a body into topsoil—is available in New Hampshire, I want to be cremated. Try the local cremation society first. It has a web page. And check the cost—the cremation starts at about $1,200, which is pennies compared to some others.

If this doesn't work, try the two local funeral homes. These also handle cremation. Neither one is unreasonably expensive—at the time of this writing the cost is roughly $2,500, but even so, it's twice as expensive as the local cremation society. Tell them that you want my ashes in a box or a bag, not in an urn.

2. The cemetery we use belongs to the town, the grave is in my name, and the town clerk and/or the town administrator will know who to ask about opening it. Ashes can be kept indefinitely—we kept Steve's mother's ashes for several months until we could take them to his father's grave—so you can wait as long as you like to deal with mine. If I die in the winter, you might want to wait until spring.

3. Our gravestone is a boulder from the edge of our field, but the company in our town that makes headstones added the names and dates, including mine, but mine is waiting for the death date. The people in that company are helpful, and it won't be too expensive because they'll only need to add four numerals for the year.

4. At some point, maybe a few days after I die (but you decide), friends and family could have a little gathering for whoever wants to come, just as we did for Steve. For Steve we had it in the barn and offered sandwiches, also stuffed eggs, which, if I say so myself, were delicious (I made them), also many kinds of cookies, a variety of soft drinks, also tea and coffee. Of course, you don't need to do any of this, but if you do, you should do it however you like.

5. You should provide an obituary for the local paper. Below is a draft I'd like you to use. Tell the editor it's this or nothing.

Elizabeth Marshall Thomas died peacefully on (*give date and keep the word "peacefully," even if it wasn't*) at age (*give my age*). She was born in Boston, Massachusetts, in 1931, was married long and happily to Stephen M. Thomas, now deceased, and is survived by their daughter, their son, two grandsons, three granddaughters, and a great-grandson. (*If other great-grandchildren appear, be sure to change "great-grandson" to "great-grandchildren" and be careful how you do this. To be sure it doesn't say "a great-grandchildren," give the number and genders of the great-grandchildren involved.*)

She and her family lived in many places, but since 1935 Peterborough was always her home. She served on town boards and committees and was the first woman in New Hampshire to serve a full term on a Board of Selectmen, a position she held for fifteen years. She never lost an election, although once when she thought she might lose, she didn't run. A few other elections were close, but she creamed her opponent in her last one. (*Keep the word "creamed."*)

She was the author of (*give number*) books, mostly nonfiction but also two novels and a Christmas story. She was probably best known for *The Hidden Life of Dogs*, which was published internationally and was on the *New York Times* bestseller list for almost a year. From it, she made enough money to buy the beach area on Cunningham Pond, which she then gave to the town. It took Town Meeting two years to accept it—some voters thought it would be used by teenagers to have sex and take drugs—but when one voter shouted, "I want to go swimming," Town Meeting accepted the gift.

Perhaps her most significant books were *The Harmless People* and *The Old Way: A Story of the First People*, as these were about the San—the precontact hunter-gatherers who were our ancestors, living on the African savanna as our species had lived before the Neolithic. During the 1950s she spent about three years among the San and was one of the last people living who had seen the culture of our ancestors—perhaps the most successful culture the world has ever known and now is essentially gone.

In lieu of flowers, please donate to the Kalahari Peoples Fund, https://www.kalahripeoples.org.

---

6. This should take care of the matter. If I was asking for a regular funeral with embalming, a fancy coffin, viewing the departed, a funeral service, a hearse to take me and a limousine to take you to the cemetery, to say nothing of opening the grave and the burial itself, you'd be lucky if it cost only $10,000. I want you to do something better with the money, like going to Tanzania to watch the wildebeest migration. I will live in your hearts, so when you do that, I'll be there. And don't worry about what I may be missing. I've already seen the wildebeest migration.

Eighteen

I 'm glad I lived when I did, and I wouldn't change it even if I could. Many people my age feel the same way. We'd lose the time period we occupied, which in my case began in 1931.

To me and many of my contemporaries, most of the current changes are appalling. In my case, because my current family members are younger than I am, I feel selfish to have had a lifetime they couldn't enjoy and to escape the troubles that will face them.

During my lifetime, precontact hunter-gatherers who lived in the Old Way were with us. Climate change was barely detectable. Few animals were threatened with extinction. The

Great Depression ended. Our country became the strongest and safest in the world. World War II happened, but we didn't start it, and we won. Japan became our ally, as did Germany, now a liberal democracy. Fascism is returning but isn't here yet. Very few people felt they needed automatic weapons, and for most of my lifetime no church would have offered blessings for the AR-15 and the AK-47, as did a church in Pennsylvania shortly after a school shooting.

And for most of my life, if not at the time of this writing, every president, Republican or Democrat, was self-controlled and sane, so I'm glad to have lived in the time of Barack Obama. During his presidency, I went to Tanzania, where almost every day, I'd meet someone who'd ask, "Who is the president of the United States?" They knew the name; they just wanted to hear me say it, so I'd say, "Barack Obama," and they'd beam. One of these people was named Baraka. I asked him what Baraka meant. He hesitated, as if slightly embarrassed, and then said it means "Blessed."

IF I COULD CHOOSE A LIFETIME, I'D PICK ONE MUCH EARLIER, maybe soon after we came down from the trees. This would have been an interesting time, but since this isn't possible, and even if it were, I wouldn't have realized that it was interesting, I'm glad of the one I have now. To me, it's been splendid, or it was until recently, and my fervent hope is that everyone, especially those I love, can say the same when they're old.

Maybe that's possible, unlikely as it seems. My mother told me that perhaps in 1917 or 1918—when she would have been in her twenties—an elderly man, probably in his eighties (thus born in about 1835), told her the world was disintegrating, going to pieces, and he didn't want to see it. But to her, the world didn't seem to be disintegrating.

When I was young, I felt the same. When we start life, what we see is the norm and we accept what we're handed. Disapproval of conditions is mainly reserved for the old when they see that things have changed.

THESE DAYS IT SEEMS UNLIKELY THAT OUR SPECIES WILL FIX climate change or end the mass extinctions, but we're good at coping, so my guess is that the next generations will become accustomed to violent hurricanes, terrible fires, and serious droughts, and some will find ways to survive them. Those in seaside communities will move to higher ground. And nobody except the scientists will know that there once were such things as wild animals. When those people are old, some may say they liked their lifetime, although that's a strange form of optimism, because the time will come, maybe sooner rather than later, when we humans join the endangered-species club.

But other species will keep going, and it's good to remember this. Every life-form that we see on earth today—every individual fern or flower, every individual beetle or sparrow, has an unbroken chain of ancestors, one after another all the way back for 3.8 billion years to a molecule in the water, and despite the many extinctions, every single one of those ancestors coped. We may go extinct with the wildlife we're erasing, but for 5 billion years, until the sun burns out, life should continue in some form.

Nineteen

Now to reveal the advantages of aging. When speaking of myself, I've described a human wreckage, so I haven't made aging seem good. And I haven't even told you that I talk to myself if I've been alone for a while, or that my left salivary gland has ceased to function, so my mouth is always dry and the gland makes a lump on my face, or that I've lost whatever coordination I had, so when I was trying to pick up some clothespins, I had trouble holding them all, so I put some in my mouth. We old people don't have enough hands, so it's a good thing we have mouths.

Even so, although I'm not hiking the Appalachian Trail and

I'm not beautiful, if you see me at a bookstore event, giving a talk and signing copies of this book for those who want them, you'll wonder if I'm the person who wrote it, because, like almost everyone my age and in my condition, most of the problems don't show.

Yet most of us have them, either some of them or all of them, just as I've described, and if you're as old as I am, you've learned to act as if you don't have them. Your hearing aids aren't noticeable, you're cogent enough that what you say makes sense (more or less), you try to walk with your back straight and your head up, but even if you're in a wheelchair or using a cane, you seem reasonably functional. That's because you are reasonably functional. The key word here is "reasonably." You are a functional elder. You've found ways to adjust, and you've also improved yourself with the wisdom you have gained from living.

THUS LIFE WHILE AGING CAN BE WONDERFUL. IT'S JUST WONDER-ful in a different way than it was when you were young. For instance, you're smarter than the younger people, but not because your brain functions better. Your brain was at its peak when you were thirty, and now that you're old, you forget people's names and lose things. But you understand the world around you more deeply and clearly. You excel at interpreting your surroundings because of all you've learned.

Young people may object to this statement. They may not believe that wrinkled old people who wobble when they walk understand things better than they do. But it's true.

For instance, as my cousin Tom puts it, from the various medical problems we experience, we receive a "memorable, if unwanted, medical education." But that's not exactly a sunbeam—our other advancements are better. We tend to be more reasonable. If we have phobias, we tend to lose them, or many of us do. We knew our phobias were unrealistic, but we had them anyway, and it's hard to believe we lose them just like we lose our glasses or our keys. But that's not impossible.

Perhaps when we lived in the trees we didn't have phobias. Fears such as fear of the dark or fear of snakes had survival value; thus it was helpful to have them, but most phobias aren't helpful now and never were. So perhaps our post-Paleolithic brains acknowledge only the Paleolithic dangers and scoff at the dangers we choose for ourselves. By the time we're old, we have enough trouble dealing with reality, so perhaps we just cancel our self-chosen fears.

I once was afraid of flying, although I had to fly sometimes, but by the time I was old, to my surprise, I had lost the fear and didn't know why. I also had a caterpillar phobia, but this also faded, perhaps because for eighty years no caterpillar harmed me, but more likely because a phobia is something we may lose as we age.

This allowed me to help three woolly bears who were on

my driveway. It happened one evening in early December, and the three little caterpillars were motionless with cold. These little creatures become tiger moths in spring, so they must get through the winter, which they do by freezing solid. It's an impressive ability, to live for several months while frozen solid (although their Arctic relatives, the woolly worms, can live for ten or fifteen years, spending the winters frozen solid). But if my woolly bears spent a winter frozen on the driveway, a car might crush them, so I picked them up and put them on my lawn in fallen leaves. These shelter many little creatures. I don't rake the leaves until spring.

Old age can make us more compassionate—another benefit—because compassion feels good. If we've had financial concerns during our long lifetime, as most of us do, we can identify with people in need and are more likely to give to charities. Or if a driver with road rage blows his horn and gives us the finger, rather than shouting at him and giving him the finger, most of us understand that he's probably under stress, which isn't our problem, and we may smile at him and drive away. Nor are we likely to get road rage ourselves. During my seventy-one years of driving, I don't believe I've ever encountered an old person with road rage.

I know several men who once were avid hunters, but as they aged, they stopped hunting, because as we grow old we think about dying and may become reluctant to take someone else's life. One famous wildlife expert, John Kulish, the author of *Bobcats Before Breakfast*, was a very successful hunter and trapper for most of his life, but then gave up hunting and trapping after watching a female otter search for her mate, whom he had trapped and killed.

I did something like this myself. When I was younger, I set traps for the mice in my office, and the traps killed them. Today, I not only let my mice live, but I provide them with a bottle cap filled with water. The experience that led to this was vaguely like that of John Kulish. I keep a bowl of water in my office for my dogs, and one morning I found a dead mouse floating in it. She had been thirsty and tried to drink, but she fell in and drowned. I could see from her nipples that she had infants somewhere, by then alone and probably suffering, and I don't want that to happen again; hence, the bottle cap. Every morning I find it almost empty, surrounded by a few mouse droppings.

I've always loved animals but didn't mind eating meat, but now that I'm old, my compassion extends to those we consume, and I'm a vegetarian. If I see a lamb chop or a steak, I picture its first owner and wonder who he or she was before being butchered.

Flying squirrels live in the attic of my office. I've been told that they can bite electric wires and start fires, and I know an expert who gets rid of these squirrels humanely by blocking their entrance with a one-way door, so that squirrels who go out can't go back in.

That seems humane, but is it really? I didn't call him. If the entrance was blocked in the spring or summer, it would keep the parent squirrels from returning to their children, and if it was blocked in the fall, it would keep the squirrels from getting the winter food they'd stored. When I was young, I might have blocked the squirrels to prevent a possible fire. Thus old age has helped me see the world in more detail and changed me for the better. Flying squirrels have lived in my attic for many years now, and we haven't had a fire.

IF BEING MORE COMPASSIONATE IS A GIFT, ANOTHER GIFT, AT least for me, is that we elders can limit ourselves as others grow up and take our places. For instance, I used to do holidays, each of which took endless work. For most of my life I did Thanksgiving for friends and family, preparing for days, cooking a large meal with mashed potatoes, nice green vegetables, a big roasted turkey, and pies for dessert, then putting an extra leaf in the dining-room table to make it big enough for ten or twelve people, covering it with a fancy tablecloth, setting out matching napkins, newly polished silverware, and fancy plates, then serving the meal, and cleaning up afterward, late into the night, no matter how tired I was by then.

But that was nothing compared to Christmas. Christmas required shopping for countless presents; also writing, addressing, and mailing countless Christmas cards; also buying a Christmas tree or finding one in the woods near my house, cutting it down and dragging it home, then adorning it with lights and ornaments, then placing a candle in each window in the house, then stringing Christmas lights outside the house, then wrapping the presents and arranging them under the tree, then hanging stockings by the fireplace where Santa would find them, and finally preparing a bounteous Christmas dinner that surpassed the Thanksgiving dinner. If Thanksgiving took days, Christmas took weeks, but I did it.

When New Year's Eve came, we'd celebrate again. More cleaning, more cooking, then staying awake until midnight in front of a television set watching thousands of people on the streets of New York waiting to see the same thing we were waiting for—a ball dropping down a pole. Ho hum. But we did it.

Today others invite me to their Thanksgiving dinners and Christmas parties. And if I'm not with them, I just go on about my business. As for New Year's Eve, I've seen that ball drop at least sixty times. Now I'm usually asleep when it's dropping, or if I'm awake I'm doing something else.

IF YOU LIVE ALONE AND GET LONELY, THAT'S TRAGIC, BUT BEING alone has advantages, and here's another plus for being old. You don't need to consider other people because there are no other people. If you don't make the bed or sweep the floor or wash the dishes right away, nobody cares. You can do what you like. No one will see you. A friend, no longer living, drank her first cocktail in the morning and drank more throughout the day. Nobody was there to judge her or tell her this was wrong, and even if someone came to her house, she was a dignified person and never seemed drunk. She was free, and she did what she wanted. (Not that constant drinking is a good idea. It was thanks to this that she died prematurely.)

But best of all, if you live alone and work at home, you get up when you like, go to bed when you like, and work without interruption. I live with dogs and cats, demanding in their own way but not as demanding as people, so my time is my own, and I can work from five o'clock in the morning until eight o'clock at night without interruption. I don't do breakfast, lunch, and dinner—I eat only when I'm hungry, thus not often—and I get a lot done in that time.

That's the bright side of being old and alone. Being busy with something you like is essential, so after I finish this book, I'll work on a novel I've started (it has a terrific beginning), or maybe I'll write that book about commas. Either project would be pleasant, and neither requires great strength.

And even if I'm confused and forgetful, even if I walk with a cane, wear glasses, hearing aids, and a pad in my pants in case I leak a little, I may also go to Thailand, where, using my cane, I'll walk five miles and see dholes. (Again, that's *Cuon alpinus*, the Asiatic version of wolves.) And when I get home I'll write about them.

So you see? Not only can you adjust to aging, you can sometimes do the things you did when you were young. You just do them with a little more equipment and in different ways, which seems easy enough, especially if age has made you smarter and more thoughtful.

But because I've become more thoughtful, I may not go to Thailand. I'd be by far the oldest person, others would need to wait for me when hiking, and I could be seen as a problem. I was on a similar wildlife safari some years ago in Kenya when one of the members was a problem—always in need, demanding constant attention from the other members—and I don't want to be like that.

Also, I have this thing about feeling light-headed and also those chest pains, and I don't yet know what causes them. (I'm still planning to see my doctor.) What if I have a stroke in Thailand? What if I have a heart attack? What if I have a stroke *and* a heart attack in Thailand?

I'd be almost eighty-eight, and the nearest hospital would be miles away. Thai doctors may not be as good as American doctors, and if I die, I'll cause a serious problem, because, unless they bury me in Thailand or feed me to the dholes, they'd have to ship my body to New Hampshire. This will be horribly expensive, extremely time-consuming, and monumentally troublesome, involving embalmment, a coffin, and probably a new plane ticket, because a dead body in a bag or a coffin would be treated as baggage and the return part of my round-trip ticket won't apply. Then there'll be some form of pickup, some method of getting me through customs, and some form of delivery.

So will I boldly go to Thailand? Or will I cautiously stay home? Bold is good unless it leads to problems. Cautious is good when you see you avoided the problems. I'll have to think hard and decide slowly. To carefully consider instead of making snap decisions is another advantage of old age.

Twenty

Drat. It took so long to write that last chapter that my vision went blurry. I'll have to end the book. Then I'll clear out my house, so my children won't need to, and be ready for that "better place." Dylan Thomas might not approve, but I won't rage against the dying of the light, because rage makes you agitated. Acceptance makes you peaceful. I'll be peacefully safe in the hearts of my children, as my dogs, cats, and family are in mine.

As I'm going, my children say they'd like to be with me. I'd like that too, so if I can, I'll die when they're nearby and have time. Then I'll be down in the ground, not in heaven or hell or in Dylan Thomas's dark night, and as for being in a better place, it's on the north side of a hill and thus better than the south side of the hill, which is a worse place. Ours is a place a fox once favored and where a bear might make a winter den. If they approve, then I will too, and I will be with those I love, even if none of us know it.

The end.

	MARSHALL	
1889	LAURENCE	1980
1898	LORNA	2002
	THOMAS	
1932	STEPHEN	2015
1931	ELIZABETH	

P.S. Did you notice the commas in this book? All the commas are important, so if by chance you didn't notice, you might want to read the book again. After all I have said about smoking, writing this book made me quit. It's bad for you.

Acknowledgments

For their help in producing this book, I'm grateful to Sy Montgomery, Nancy Folsom, Deana Darby, Kendra Boileau, Shannon Welch, Ann Moru, Tom Bryant, Howard Nelson, Jennifer Lyons, Megan Biesele, Paula Gordon, Janice Frost, and anonymous sources.

Sy Montgomery is the best friend anyone could have. Just about every time I talked with her, I'd get a great idea from something she said, and I'd instantly note it in my little notebook. She also read drafts of this book and made important suggestions.

Nancy Folsom is not only a dear friend, but is also an RN

who for much of her life has been a caregiver, most recently as a hospice nurse. She knows everything there is to know about nursing issues, also about aging issues, and she has been wonderfully helpful. She's also been supportive of the work I try to do. She had shirts made for Sy and me with pictures of the book we wrote together on them. That book is *Tamed and Untamed: Close Encounters of the Animal Kind*. Nancy also had a shirt made with a picture of my next book, *The Hidden Life of Life: A Walk Through the Reaches of Time*. I wear these shirts with gratitude and pride.

I was fortunate to talk with Deana Darby, whose insightful knowledge of transitioning from life to death was exceptionally helpful. I wish I'd known earlier that she was a doula, and perhaps I did, but I thought doulas helped only with birth. If I'd known the truth when my husband was dying, I would have asked for Deana's help. Everything would have been different and better.

Kendra Boileau was the editor of *The Hidden Life of Life*, published by Pennsylvania State University Press as part of the Animalibus book series, which I'm honored to be part of. (Yes, I ended the sentence with a preposition. Kendra wouldn't have done that.) She read the penultimate draft of this book, not professionally, just out of friendship and the kindness of her heart, and offered suggestions, all of which were important and all of which I gratefully took.

Shannon Welch is now my editor, and what a wonderful experience this is for me. Rather than writing "STET" by her proposed changes, however few, I make the changes, not only because she's right, but because I hope to please her. Not every writer feels this way about an editor.

Ann Moru was the copy editor for this book and I hope will be for any other books I write. Not every writer feels this way about a copy editor. But here's the hard part. While I was seeing myself as a comma expert and boasting shamelessly, I learned (groan) that Ann was a better comma expert. Humbled as I am, I'm also grateful because, thanks to what I learned from Ann, at last I see myself not just as a comma expert but as a super comma expert. Also, this book had a few embarrassing errors that had nothing to do with word choice or punctuation, but Ann found and fixed them just the same. For instance, do you see "Chapter 19" in the following paragraph? I had it wrongly as "Chapter 18." Ann found the mistake without even a hint that something was wrong. I don't know how she did this unless she has the world's best memory, or unless she fact-checked, at least mentally, the entire manuscript. I would not have been able to do this myself and I wrote the book!

Tom Bryant is my cousin. He's very supportive, he made original suggestions for subject matter, he helped with mathematical issues, he provided the statement in Chapter 19 about elders receiving "a memorable, if unwanted, medical education," and also the sentence in the Introduction that presents a large number in the form of feet, yards, and miles.

Howard Nelson is a gifted poet, but he also offers important observations in prose. I thank him for the insightful quote about his canoe-camping experience with his adult children and young grandchildren, when he wondered if he was still the expedition leader or was "transitioning into the old guy they take along." As a summary of aging, that's hard to beat.

Jennifer Lyons is my agent. I didn't have an agent for this book, and then, as if by a miracle, she blossomed into my life. It took her about a nanosecond to join me with Shannon and therefore with a publisher, and I hope she doesn't tire of my worries and questions because I hope to be her client for the rest of my life.

Megan Biesele, a lifelong friend, is an anthropologist who speaks Ju/'hoan fluently and has spent many years among the San. She's the founder and manager of the Kalahari Peoples Fund, and has given me continuing information about the Ju/'hoansi. She also told me how to spell the Ju/'hoan words used here. There's little about the Ju/'hoansi that Megan doesn't know.

Paula Gordon is also a dear friend who not only had me on her television show and offers good suggestions that help with things I'm struggling with, but told me about natural organic reduction, which if not for her would not have been mentioned.

Janice Frost has been my assistant since Bella died. She understands my problems and can find things for me because she knows where I might have left them. She cares for my dogs and cats when I'm away, and all of them love her. Chapek, my Chihuahua, would rather have her than me as his person. She's a loving, caring woman and as for housekeeping, I wouldn't even try without her.

And I'm profoundly grateful to my anonymous sources. You know who you are, dear people, but the information you provided could cast negative light on certain enterprises and might tempt others to place blame. You will live in my heart.

I've conjured a colleague named Bigfoot. I'm not at all grateful to him. He was asked to read the book and identify mistakes but he didn't do this, so it's his fault, not mine, if they're here.

About the Author

Nancy Folsom

One of the most widely read American writers about the natural world, Elizabeth Marshall Thomas has written fifteen books during her half-century-long career. Her fifth book, *The Hidden Life of Dogs*, spent a year on the *New York Times* bestseller list, and along with her book on cats, *Tribe of Tiger*, and her novel *Reindeer Moon*, was an international bestseller. Thomas holds a BA from Radcliffe College and an MA from The George Washington University. Born in Boston in 1931, she now lives on her family's former farm in New Hampshire.